In Your Corner

WITH KERRY PHARR

A Boxing Trainer's Tales
from
Ali to Holyfield

KERRY PHARR

IN YOUR CORNER WITH KERRY PHARR

First Edition

Subtitle: A Boxing Trainer's Tales from Ali to Holyfield

All Scripture quotations, unless otherwise indicated, are taken from the Holy Bible, New International Version®, NIV®. Copyright ©1973, 1978, 1984, 2011 by Biblica, Inc.™ Used by permission of Zondervan. All rights reserved worldwide. www.zondervan.com The "NIV" and "New International Version" are trademarks registered in the United States Patent and Trademark Office by Biblica, Inc.™

This book and its contents are wholly the creation and intellectual property of Kerry Pharr.

This book may not be reproduced in whole or in part, by electronic process or any other means, without written permission of the author.

ISBN: 979-8-343783-39-1

Copyright © 2024 by Kerry Pharr

All Rights Reserved

Contents

Thomas "Hit Man" Hearns vs. "The Bull"	1
Tommy "The Duke" Morrison & Rising Heavyweight Keith McKnight...	11
"Tyson's Gonna Knock You Out, Adam!"	15
Kerry Pharr: Boxing's Elusive Dream............................	23
Meeting the Great Jack Dempsey	27
Rocky Graziano Nearly Rips My Chin Off......................	30
Watching Muhammad Ali Train at Navy Pier	32
Jimmy Heair: All He Has Left Is Courage	39
The Most Notorious Fight of All: Luis Resto vs. Billy Collins	46
Darrell "Fast Fists" Fuller	51
Hall of Fame Matchmaker Teddy Brenner	59
"Fast Fists" Fuller Defends Title Against Gary Hinton ...	62
The Murder of Donald Bowers......................................	64
Diamond Jim MacDonald	68
Tim Johnson vs. David Bates: Dueling Head Butts	75
Keith McKnight	83
Benito "Baby" Ortiz: From the Ring to Redemption.......	96
Eddie Futch's First Boxer: Luthur Burgess	101
The Tragic Tale of Big John Tate	107
Mark Gastineau: Pro Football's King of the Sack	113
Slaves of the Sugar Plantation	118
Boxing's Treacherous Road	123

Dave Wolf, the Epitome of a Great Boxing Manager 129
Fight the Good Fight 132
From Death to Life 136

— 1 —

Thomas "Hit Man" Hearns vs. "The Bull"

As the electrifying sound of music filled the 50,000-seat Aloha Stadium in Honolulu, Hawaii, a palpable energy swept through the crowd. The legendary five-time world champion, Thomas "Hit Man" Hearns, made his way toward the ring, flanked by his entourage. Hearns, known for his devastating knockouts, had carved his name into boxing history with victories over the likes of Pipino Cuevas, Dennis Andries, and the iconic Roberto Duran, whom he demolished in just two rounds. He had outboxed Wilfredo Benitez, the youngest ever to win a world title, and nearly defeated the great Sugar Ray Leonard in their first encounter. The mere mention of Hearns' name sent chills down the spines of even the most hardened fighters.

But on this afternoon, it wasn't a celebrated champion or a well-known contender standing in the ring awaiting the "Hit Man." Instead, it was Ken "The Bull" Atkin, an unknown boxer from Smyrna,

Tennessee, whom I had managed and trained throughout his career. A fighter with a limited amateur background, Atkin had started boxing at the late age of 19. With only twelve amateur bouts under his belt, he lacked the polish of those with extensive careers. Yet, what Atkin lacked in experience, he more than made up for with sheer toughness and an indomitable spirit. His nickname, "The Bull," earned during his junior high football days for his charging ways, was a fitting moniker for a man who never backed down.

Atkin's dream of stepping into BIG-TIME BOXING materialized when the infamous boxing promoter Harold Smith called me, searching for an opponent for Hearns. In the boxing world, the term "opponent" often comes with a grim connotation. An opponent is not expected to win; they are brought in to give the star fighter some work, a human punching bag to bolster the champion's record. Smith, clearly aware of this dynamic, asked me over the phone, "You're not going to bring your guy in and upset my fighter, are you?"

Though our plan was to give it everything we had, I didn't want to say anything that might make Smith reconsider and find another opponent. So, I played along. "Harold, you know the odds of us beating Hearns are slim to none," I said, earning a chuckle from Smith as he concluded our conversation.

We approached the fight with a deliberate strategy: to embrace the role of the underdog until the very moment the bell rang. Our hope was that Hearns would underestimate Atkin, neglect his training, and give us the best possible chance to pull off a miracle.

For many boxers without national amateur titles or Olympic experience, opportunities like this come along maybe once or twice in a lifetime—if at all. Most professional fighters never reach the multi-million-dollar paydays that make headlines. An "opportunity fight" like this one is the stuff of dreams for underdog fighters, much like the fictional Rocky Balboa. When that opportunity comes, you grab it with both hands.

Atkin didn't see himself as just an opponent. He envisioned himself as a winner, not a sacrificial lamb. He wasn't intimidated by Hearns or his reputation. To him, this was the chance of a lifetime, and he trained with the intensity of a man possessed. While most boxers prepare for a 10-round fight with five miles of roadwork per day, Atkin was pushing himself to eight or even ten miles. He went fifteen rounds in sparring sessions three times a week, despite the fight only being scheduled for ten rounds.

Hearns, on the other hand, was already looking ahead to his bout with Virgil Hill for the light-heavyweight championship later that year. As we stood in the ring, we watched the "Hit Man" and his entourage emerge at the far end of the stadium, an army of supporters rallying around their champion. They bounced to the music, shouting encouragements as they marched toward us.

In stark contrast, Atkin had no entourage, no fanfare. It was just him, Keith McKnight, and me standing in the corner, feeling outnumbered and alone, like we were in a dogfight with a pit bull and his pack ready to tear us apart. Hearns was that pit bull, and his crew pointed at us like we were prey, shouting, "Sic 'em!"

Ken Atkin vs. Tommy "Hit Man" Hearns

When Hearns entered the ring, it was as if a military assault squad had breached our defenses. The crowd erupted in thunderous applause as the champion glided around the ring, his eyes locked onto

Atkin. He moved with the grace of a maestro, his regal robe swirling as he twirled around, his entourage hollering instructions and encouragement.

For a brief moment, doubt crept into my mind. I couldn't help but wonder if I had made a grave mistake in matching Atkin with Hearns. I feared for my fighter's safety and silently prayed for his well-being. But Atkin, completely unfazed by the psychological warfare, snapped me out of my thoughts with a confident smile.

"What? Is all of that supposed to scare me or something?" he asked.

The anxiety before a big fight is intense—your stomach churns, and your mind races with a hundred thoughts. But once the bell rings, everything calms down. The focus shifts entirely to the task at hand.

In most fights, the first round is a cautious feeling-out process. Fighters meet in the center of the ring, testing each other, searching for openings. But we knew that strategy wouldn't work against Hearns. I believed the safest place for Atkin was right on Hearns' chest, forcing a close-quarters fight. Just before the bell rang, I leaned in and told Atkin, "You've got ten seconds to get on his chest."

The 5'7" Atkin showed no respect for Hearns' power or reputation. As soon as the bell rang, he charged across the ring, closing the distance and engaging the 6'1" champion in a brawl. Hearns backed into a neutral corner, but with the precision of a master, he slipped to Atkin's left shoulder, then to the right, and unleashed a series of ferocious left hooks into Atkin's midsection. These punches would have crippled many fighters, but Atkin, in the best shape of his life, absorbed them without flinching.

At ringside, former World Welterweight Champion Carlos Palomino was calling the fight as a television commentator. "Boy, this Atkin kid is tough! He doesn't believe he is an opponent. He came to win," Palomino exclaimed.

Hearns pivoted out of the corner and fired his lightning-fast jab. Swish! The jab snapped Atkin's head back, but he ducked under the next shot and pressed forward, pushing Hearns against the ropes. Then, Atkin delivered his best punch of the fight—a picture-perfect right hand that landed squarely on Hearns' chin.

Palomino shouted, "Man, Atkin just hit Hearns with a really good shot!"

The punch sent Hearns reeling into the ropes, where he quickly regained his balance and covered up as the bell rang, ending the first round.

Afterwards, Hearns threw one punch after another, trying to end the fight with his signature right hand, the same punch that had felled champions and legends alike. But Atkin, employing a Detroit-style shoulder roll, slipped under the punch each time, determined to stay in the fight.

For six grueling minutes, Atkin went toe-to-toe

with one of the greatest boxers in history, giving as good as he got. But midway through the third round, Hearns landed a punch above Atkin's left eye, opening a deep cut. The referee, concerned about the injury, called the ringside physician to examine the gash. After a brief inspection, the doctor advised the referee to stop the fight, and Hearns was awarded a third-round technical knockout.

Ken Atkin vs. Tommy "Hit Man" Hearns

Later that year, Hearns went on to capture the light-heavyweight world championship from Virgil Hill. Atkin, on the other hand, continued his bi-vocational career, working full-time during the day as a police officer and training as a boxer at night. Atkin ultimately won the World Boxing Federation's light heavyweight title. While Hearns retired a multi-millionaire, Atkin remained true to his roots, working his day job to pay the bills.

Though the odds were stacked against him, Atkin displayed the heart and courage to stand toe-to-toe with one of the greatest boxers in the sport's history. Few gave Atkin a chance to last even one round against Hearns. But he defied expectations, battling the "Hit Man" on even terms for three rounds without ever being knocked down or out. He faced the heat, stood his ground, and refused to quit.

Weeks after the fight, Hearns graciously signed a photo of the two of them in the ring, writing, "No Rematch, Thomas Hearns." It was a testament to the respect Atkin had earned in those three unforgettable rounds.

After the Hearns fight, Atkin continued his career for another several years. On October 23, 1993, he competed for and secured the World Boxing Federation Light-Heavyweight title, defeating Mexico's Carlos Cantu with a fifth-round knockout at Nashville's Municipal Auditorium. Unfortunately, multiple injuries eventually forced Atkin to retire with a record of 30 wins and 5 losses.

Atkin's Sister Murdered

Ken's life outside the ring has been far tougher than any battle he faced inside it. His sister and best friend, Melissa "Missy" Atkin, was tragically murdered by her boyfriend, Larry Scott Reynolds, during a custody battle over their son, Lucas, on December 16, 2007. Reynolds ambushed Melissa outside her home in Murfreesboro, Tennessee, on that fateful night. Armed with a pistol, he forced Melissa inside, tied her hands behind her back, stripped her from the waist down, and executed her with four shots to the back of her head.

Missy, Ken and Larry Atkin

Reynolds was eventually found guilty and is now serving a life sentence in prison. While the Atkin family saw justice served, the murder left them shattered. Missy's parents, Doug and Linda, now in their eighties, have spent nearly two decades grieving their daughter's loss while raising her son, Lucas, as their own. Linda Atkin has found solace in Lucas, saying, "He's a joy, and he makes us laugh. He even dusts. We're blessed. We lost something beyond belief, but we were given something the same way." Lucas, now an adult, works as the head of the produce department at a large grocery store chain. He, his grandparents, and Ken currently live together in the same house.

Missy's murder was especially hard on Ken. As a fighter, lifelong police officer, and expert marksman, his first instinct was to seek revenge—an eye-for-an-eye type of justice. Initially, the family didn't know who the killer was, and Reynolds pretended to grieve alongside them. However, as evidence mounted against him, it became clear he was the perpetrator. Doug and Linda pleaded with Ken not to do anything rash, and ultimately, Ken allowed the law to bring Reynolds to justice.

In a television interview ten years later, Ken confided that the hardest thing he ever had to do was learn to forgive his sister's murderer. But he did. The weight of being a police officer, coupled with the trauma of Missy's murder, took a heavy toll on Ken. He has struggled with serious health issues, including prostate cancer, and has undergone over 30 surgeries. However, Ken Atkin remains "The Bull."

— 2 —

Tommy "The Duke" Morrison & Rising Heavyweight Keith McKnight

In the winter of 1994, I received a call from International Boxing matchmaker Sean Gibbons, a man with deep roots in the sport—being the cousin of former Lightweight Boxing Champion and beloved commentator Sean O'Grady. Gibbons had an intriguing offer to match Ken Merritt, a tough but limited heavyweight I managed, against former heavyweight champion Tommy "The Duke" Morrison in a televised fight. At that time, Merritt had already faced the likes of former champions Lou Savarese in Reno, Nevada, and Brian Nielsen in Denmark, albeit with losses. As a manager juggling five different heavyweights, the opportunity for a journeyman like Merritt to get one last shot at glory on national television was a dream come true.

Merritt was eager to step into the ring with Morrison on February 7, 1995. Gibbons sweetened the deal by offering to feature my rising prospect,

Keith McKnight, in the undercard's opening bout against Gary Butler from Tyler, Texas. McKnight made a sensational statement that night, delivering a first-round knockout over Butler—though the victory came at a cost, as he broke his hand during the fight and was sidelined for several months.

Keith McKnight scores a knockout

As impressive as McKnight's performance was, Morrison proved why he was a former champion by delivering a devastating knockout to Merritt in the very first round of their bout. In the dressing room afterward, a reflective Merritt admitted, "I really thought I could beat Morrison—until I got hit and felt his power." Despite the outcome, Merritt walked away with a decent payday and, more importantly, without any serious injuries. Three months later, he hung up his gloves for good, ending his career with a professional record of 14-8 after securing a unanimous decision over Tim St. Clair in a six-round fight.

For Team McKnight, there was a silver lining. With his slick boxing style and size comparable to Lennox Lewis, McKnight was well-positioned for future opportunities. Later that year, I got another call from Gibbons, this time asking if McKnight could join Morrison's training camp as the chief sparring partner in preparation for Morrison's upcoming bout against Lennox Lewis for the Heavyweight Championship of the World in October. McKnight spent six grueling weeks in camp, helping Morrison sharpen his skills.

Our relationship with Gibbons led to another opportunity when he later enlisted Warren Williams, another one of my fighters, to serve as a sparring partner for one of Morrison's final fights. Tragically, shortly after Williams returned home from camp, we received the devastating news that Morrison had been diagnosed with HIV, leading to the cancellation of his fight. Gibbons called to inform me of the diagnosis and advised that Williams should get tested to ensure he hadn't contracted the virus during their sessions. Ever the self-effacing humorist, Williams quipped, "I don't know why they want me to get a blood test—because the only blood shed while I sparred Morrison was mine."

Heavyweight Contender Joe Mesi poses with Warren Williams at Mesi vs. McKnight weigh-in

Tommy Morrison passed away from complications related to HIV on September 1, 2013, at the age of 44. Warren Williams, who fought his battles both in and out of the ring, succumbed to diabetes in November of 2018 at the age of 56. Their stories, intertwined with the brutality and camaraderie of the sport, serve as a stark reminder of the highs and lows that come with the life of a fighter.

— 3 —

"Tyson's Gonna Knock You Out, Adam!"

When Melvin Richards first brought his 8-year-old son Adam to the boxing gym, no one could have guessed the storm that was about to brew. Adam was short and chubby, an unlikely candidate for the sport. But beneath that soft exterior was a heart forged from the toughest steel. Raised on a diet of grit, determination, and the creed to "be tough," Adam was thrown into the deep end from day one. With no opponents his age to spar with, he faced older, stronger, and far more experienced boys. This baptism by fire would shape him into a relentless fighter with an unyielding spirit.

By the time Adam was in his early teens, his boxing career was unconventional, to say the least. Unable to find anyone his size, he took on grown men in exhibitions. And though these bouts were unofficial, Adam made a habit of delivering his own brand of punishment. Anger was his fuel. If an opponent got the better of him, Adam didn't just fight back—he fought with the fury of a tempest, sometimes with tears in his eyes, but always with the heart of a lion.

One thing was clear: Adam was no ordinary kid. He was tenacious, aggressive, and incredibly tough. But beyond the boxing ring, he was a young man with a code. Once, a high school peer made vile comments that hurt a female classmate. Without a second thought, Adam stepped in, warning the offender that any more disrespect would be met with a reckoning. He was a protector, a friend to the defenseless, and a warrior in and out of the ring.

Adam was a natural southpaw, but I trained Adam to fight right-handed, turning him into what's known in boxing as a "converted southpaw." This technique gave Adam a devastating left hook, just like the legendary Joe Frazier. And so, Adam honed his craft, learning to throw that hook with all his weight behind it, his wrist curled inward for maximum impact.

At age 13 and 14, Adam claimed two national championships almost by default, with few opponents to challenge him. But it wasn't until the summer of 1995, at the National Junior Olympics, that Adam faced his first real test—a towering 6'5" Native American boxer from Minnesota, aptly named Thunder. Adam lost that bout by decision, but the fire within him only burned hotter.

The following year, Adam hit a growth spurt,

shooting up to 6'1". With his newfound height came a terrifying new power. Opponents who had once laughed at the chubby kid were now left sprawling on the canvas, knocked out cold by Adam's thunderous left hook. As he bulldozed his way through the local and regional tournaments, Adam's reputation began to grow, but so did the skepticism. He was still soft and flabby, and many underestimated him based on his appearance.

Kerry Pharr prepping 16-year-old Adam Richards

When Adam arrived at Northern Michigan University for the national championships, he was a virtual unknown. He won his first fight by knockout, but no one noticed. All eyes were on Leonard Childs, a 16-year-old with the physique of a Greek god and the power to match. Childs was the spitting image of "Iron" Mike Tyson, the youngest man to ever win the world heavyweight title. It wasn't long before the crowd started calling him "Tyson," and the hype was off the charts.

Childs won his first bout by knockout, and the buzz only intensified. He looked unstoppable, a destroyer in the making. Adam, on the other hand, kept quietly winning, knocking out one opponent after another. But the cruel taunts from the other boxers were relentless. "Tyson's gonna knock you out, Adam," they sneered. "Tyson's gonna knock you out, Adam..." The chant echoed in his ears, a cruel refrain that only fueled his determination.

In the third round of the tournament, Adam and Childs were on a collision course. Childs faced Thunder, the same boxer who had defeated Adam the year before. But this time, Childs knocked Thunder out cold, solidifying his status as the tournament favorite. The media swarmed Childs, hailing him as the second coming of Tyson, while Adam remained in the shadows, overlooked and underestimated.

The pressure on Adam was immense. This wasn't just a fight; it was a battle against the world's expectations. No one believed he had a chance against Childs, and the weight of that doubt bore down on him. But Adam wasn't one to back down. Babe Ruth once said, "It's hard to beat a person who never gives up," and Adam embodied that spirit to the fullest.

As the finals approached, I could see the tension etched on Adam's face. This was his moment, his chance to prove everyone wrong. I tried to calm him, to remind him of the hours of training, the sparring sessions with seasoned professionals, and the devastating power of his left hook. We prayed together, asking for strength and protection. I knew Adam had what it took, but it was up to him to seize the moment.

When the day of the finals arrived, the arena buzzed with anticipation. Childs, the fearsome "Tyson," was the clear favorite. But as Adam climbed into the ring, there was a quiet confidence about him. He was ready.

The bell rang, and the two fighters met in the center of the ring. For a moment, they circled each other, feeling each other out. Then, with the precision of a seasoned veteran, Adam unleashed his left hook. It connected flush with Childs' jaw, and the mighty "Tyson" crumpled to the canvas like a house of cards. The crowd was stunned into silence. Adam had knocked him out in the first minute of the first round. One punch was all it took to shatter the myth of invincibility that had surrounded Childs.

Adam Richards was the new national champion, having knocked out every single opponent in his path. The kid everyone had ignored had just delivered one of the most shocking upsets in amateur boxing history. But this was no fluke. Adam went on to win the national championship again in 1997, once more knocking out every opponent he faced. He joined the ranks of legends, matching the feat of none other than the real Mike Tyson.

As the years went by, Adam's power only grew. He became a force to be reckoned with, a warrior in every sense of the word.

As a professional boxer, Adam Richards was promoted by boxing manager Chris Rowland and trained by the legendary Ronnie Shields, a man who had guided the great heavyweight champion Evander Holyfield. Training alongside Holyfield in the famed Houston gym, Adam became one of the champion's regular sparring partners, absorbing not just the punches but the lessons of a master.

But Adam's toughness wasn't forged solely in the boxing ring. In high school, he was a standout lineman for the Riverdale Warriors in Murfreesboro, Tennessee, where the brutal clashes on the football field added to the wear and tear on his body. The relentless battles—whether on the gridiron, as an amateur boxer, or while trading blows with a heavyweight legend—took a silent toll. Over time, these countless collisions contributed to a tragic outcome: chronic traumatic encephalopathy (CTE), a brain disorder that haunts many athletes who have suffered repeated head injuries.

CTE is a progressive brain disorder caused by

repeated head trauma. It primarily impacts athletes involved in contact sports but can also affect military personnel and others who engage in activities with a high risk of head injuries. Currently, CTE can only be definitively diagnosed through an autopsy after death.

Despite the toll on his body, Richards built an impressive career, amassing a 23-3 professional record and earning a spot as a top ten world-rated cruiserweight. His journey led him to Germany, where he faced Marco Huck for the WBO Cruiserweight Championship of the world. But the dream of a world title was cut short in the third round when Huck landed a devastating elbow to Richards' skull, opening a massive gash that forced the referee to stop the fight via TKO.

After hanging up his gloves, Adam transitioned to life as a home builder in The Woodlands, Texas. He found love and stability with his beautiful wife, Chevon, and their handsome son, Gavin. But every morning, Adam wakes up with the echoes of his past battles—severe headaches and the lingering trauma, the symptoms of CTE.

Now, with the same determination that once propelled him in the ring, Adam is driven by a new mission: to shed light on the countless athletes who silently suffer from brain injury, the byproduct of careers spent enduring blow after blow.

Sadly, boxing—a sport that demands so much

from its warriors—offers no safety net, no health insurance, no pension fund for those who gave their all in the ring. Adam Richards, like many before him, faces the harsh reality that after the lights have dimmed and the crowds have gone home, the battle is far from over.

Adam Richards and Kerry Pharr in 2024

— 4 —

Kerry Pharr: Boxing's Elusive Dream

From the moment I could sit in front of a television, boxing captivated me. Friday nights were sacred, dedicated to the *Gillette Cavalcade of Sports*, where I watched in awe as warriors battled in the ring. My passion for the sport was more than just a fleeting interest; it was an obsession, driven by stories of grit and glory. My best friend, Danny Taylor, shared that passion, but he had something I didn't—a direct link to the world of boxing through his cousin, Larry Freeman, a three-time Golden Gloves Champion. Larry opened the doors to the world of boxing for Danny and me, and we eagerly stepped through.

Our local gym in Kenosha, Wisconsin, was only open three months a year, just in time to prepare for the Annual Golden Gloves tournament. Boxing there felt almost seasonal, like baseball or basketball. With no professional boxers in our town and limited time in the gym, it was tough to compete with fighters who trained year-round in cities like Chicago and Milwaukee. Despite the challenges, I boxed on and off throughout my teenage years, participating in local club shows and fighting in the Golden Gloves. But without a dedicated trainer to guide me, I remained just an ordinary, tough brawler—someone who could take a beating and keep going.

At 20, I married my childhood sweetheart and decided to chase my dream of becoming a professional fighter. I began driving to Milwaukee and Chicago to spar with pros, hoping to refine my skills. A chance meeting at Del Porter's gym with Vidal Flores, a Mexican light-heavyweight who had fought top-tier opponents, was exactly what I needed. I asked Vidal if I could spar with him, and for the next six months, I let him beat me up nearly every day. It was brutal, but quitting was never an option. I loved the sport too much. Slowly but surely, I improved. I began sparring with other amateurs and found that they could hardly land a punch on me.

One day, Mike Olson walked into the gym—a talented boxer who had defeated me in my last amateur fight. He asked if I wanted to spar, and I jumped at the chance. When the bell rang, I dominated the same fighter who had beaten me a year earlier. It was a turning point—I was finally learning how to box, and I dared to hope that a professional career was within reach.

But then Vidal, at 36, lost a fight and decided to

retire. Without his guidance, I felt adrift. I switched to another gym in Milwaukee, sparring with Billy Goodwin, a local middleweight pro, and even Eddie Brooks, one of Muhammad Ali's sparring partners. Eddie was a heavyweight, far too big for me, but he saw something in me and took me under his wing. Still, I knew deep down that I had started too late. I was an ordinary boxer who had become serious about the sport long after most fighters had already made their mark.

Former Heavyweight Champ Jimmy Ellis and Kerry Pharr

A professional boxing career was the best thing that never happened to me. Beyond the bright lights and television cameras, the harsh reality is that most boxers barely earn enough to get by. The glamour of the sport is reserved for a select few, while nearly all fighters hold down full-time day jobs to support their dream of becoming a champion, while training late into the night. Only about two percent of professional boxers ever see the million-dollar paydays you hear about. The rest face a grueling grind with no insurance, no pension, and no benefits—a brutal tradeoff in the pursuit of glory.

Life pulled me in another direction. I landed a great sales job with a national company, providing for my family but leaving little time for the gym. My dream of becoming a professional boxer was slipping away, even though I tried to keep it alive whenever I could. My last serious attempt at going pro didn't happen until I was in my thirties. It was then that I realized my dream was over, but another opportunity awaited. I could take the knowledge and passion I had for boxing and pour it into training young fighters, helping them achieve the dreams I once had.

— 5 —

Meeting the Great Jack Dempsey

After landing a job with a nationally recognized garment manufacturer, I was sent to New York City for a week of sales training. My days were spent in a classroom, but my nights had a different purpose—I was on a mission to meet the legendary heavyweight champion, Jack Dempsey, at his restaurant.

Dempsey's on Broadway in NYC

One late afternoon, I finally spotted him. Dempsey, his wife, and another gentleman were seated at a table. With a mixture of nerves and excitement, I approached and introduced myself. Despite being around 76 years old at the time, Dempsey—born in the same year as my grandfather, 1895—was gracious and kind. To my surprise and delight, they invited me to join them.

**Jack Dempsey Heavyweight Boxing Champion
1919-1926**

They couldn't help but chuckle at how starstruck I was. Dempsey, ever the charmer, joked that he was more of a lover than a fighter. He reminisced about his days as the world's heavyweight champion, sharing stories of how, in the 1920s, you could walk into a restaurant and order anything you wanted for just twenty-five cents. Whether it was steak, ribs, or fish, they'd cook it just the way you liked.

Dempsey's restaurant had a full-time photographer, and I eagerly paid five dollars to have my picture taken with him. About a week after returning home, an 8x10 black-and-white photograph arrived in the mail—there I was, sitting with the Manasa Mauler himself. Sadly, I lost that photo years ago, but the memory of meeting the great Jack Dempsey is a thrill I'll never forget.

— 6 —

Rocky Graziano Nearly Rips My Chin Off

After leaving Dempsey's, I set out across New York City on a mission to find another boxing legend, Rocky Graziano. I had asked around the restaurant, and someone pointed me in the direction of his apartment building. Graziano, immortalized by Paul Newman in the movie *Somebody Up There Likes Me*, was someone I wasn't going to leave New York without meeting.

I waited outside his building until nearly midnight, determined to catch a glimpse of the former middleweight champion. Finally, Rocky and his wife returned from a night out. As they approached, I gathered my nerve and introduced myself, expressing what an honor it was to meet him. Rocky, clearly in good spirits after a few drinks, turned to his wife and said, "Go on upstairs, babe. I'll be up in a few minutes."

Rocky Graziano, Middleweight
World Champion, 1947-1948

Despite being a little tipsy, Rocky was warm and friendly, willing to chat. I mentioned that I also boxed as a middleweight and, half-jokingly, asked him if he thought I could ever win the world middleweight championship. With a grin, he grabbed my chin—firmly enough to make me wonder if he might rip it off—and said, "If you get in shape."

He released my chin, and we exchanged goodnights. It was a brief encounter, but one I would remember as my meeting with the great Rocky Graziano.

— 7 —

Watching Muhammad Ali Train at Navy Pier

Growing up just fifty miles north of Chicago, I often found myself in the city, especially at the old CYO gym just west of downtown. One beautiful spring day in 1971, my friend Larry Freeman and I drove down from Wisconsin to witness the legendary Muhammad Ali train at Mayor Daley's Navy Pier gym. The gym, located at the end of the pier—an impressive structure stretching over half a mile into Lake Michigan—was the perfect setting to see "The Greatest" in action.

Ali had been forced out of boxing for three years due to his refusal to be inducted into the U.S. Army during the Vietnam War, famously stating, "I ain't got no quarrel with them Vietcong." Ali was convicted of draft evasion, sentenced to five years in prison, fined $10,000, and banned from boxing for three years. However, he avoided prison time as his case was appealed. Upon his return, he faced Jerry

Quarry, a perennial contender who, in any other era, might have been a world champion. Ali, too big, fast, and skillful, stopped Quarry in the third round, showcasing his unmatched talent. This was followed by a tough bout against Oscar Bonavena, which Ali won by knockout in the 15th round.

However, the defining fight came on March 8, 1971—the "Battle of the Century"—where Ali suffered the first loss of his career in a 15-round unanimous decision to Smokin' Joe Frazier. The fight, which was voted the *Ring Magazine* "Fight of the Year," solidified Frazier's victory with a sensational knockdown of Ali in the final round. Despite the loss, Ali earned immense respect for his resilience, and the fight went down as one of the greatest in boxing history. Just a few months later, on June 28, the U.S. Supreme Court overturned his draft evasion conviction.

Ali eventually avenged his loss to Frazier, beating him twice more, including the legendary "Thrilla in Manila" in 1975—a fight so brutal that Ali described it as a near-death experience. All three bouts between Ali and Frazier were voted Fight of the Year by *Ring Magazine*.

In the spring of 1971, after the first Frazier fight, Ali returned to the gym to prepare for a summer match against his boyhood friend and former sparring partner, Jimmy Ellis. Ellis, who was two years older, had beaten Ali in an amateur bout. Ali was training in Chicago at Mayor Daley's Navy Pier gym on the shore of Lake Michigan.

Ali, born Cassius Clay, had won an Olympic gold medal as a light heavyweight in 1960 in Rome. After defeating the formidable Sonny Liston in 1964 to claim his first heavyweight title, Clay joined the Nation of Islam and changed his name to Muhammad Ali. He was handsome, flashy, cocky, and incredibly gifted—a combination that fascinated and, at times, confounded people. Although many people didn't like the brash young fighter, you couldn't deny Ali's extraordinary skill and athleticism. His speed and mobility in the ring were unmatched, and he could dismantle even the most powerful heavyweights in the blink of an eye. His mantra, "Float like a butterfly, sting like a bee," coined by his handler Drew "Bundini" Brown, perfectly encapsulated his unique abilities.

My friend Larry, who had won the local Golden Gloves championship three years in a row, was a sharp judge of boxing talent. Larry had an uncanny knack for picking fight winners and saw something special in Ali. He decided early on to bet on Ali in every fight throughout his career, a decision that paid off as Ali proved to be a one-of-a-kind athlete.

Before Ali, boxers were usually polite and civil. But Ali burst onto the scene like a hurricane, not only predicting his victories but boldly declaring the very round he would knock out his opponent. His brashness earned him the nickname "Louisville Lip," but he backed up every word he said. As his rival Ken Norton put it, "Ali was a showman. He brought the eyes of the world toward boxing. But he could back up what he said."

Ali grew up in segregated Louisville, Kentucky, an experience that deeply impacted him. Despite winning an Olympic gold medal, he wasn't welcomed as a hero in his hometown. According to one story, after being refused service at a Louisville diner, he threw his Olympic medal into the Ohio River. This searing injustice fueled his drive to stand up against the establishment and advocate for his people.

His rivalry with Joe Frazier was one of the most intense in boxing history. Ali belittled Frazier, calling him an "Uncle Tom" and even questioning his appearance. This animosity lingered for years, although Ali later expressed regret for some of the things he said. Frazier, Ali acknowledged, brought out the best in him.

Ali's impact extended far beyond the boxing ring. He angered and frightened his opponents, as well as the establishment, with his bold declarations of pride and independence. In an era of social change, Ali's defiance resonated deeply, particularly with Black Americans. His outspokenness during a time of racial tension in America made him a hero to many, especially those who had long been voiceless.

For Black Americans, he was a symbol of pride and resistance; for the rest of the world, he was simply "The Greatest."

Kerry Pharr, Muhammad Ali (Nov. 1971)

That day at Navy Pier, about 100 fans, including Larry and me, gathered to watch Ali train. After his workout, he entertained us by shooting hook shots from half court on the basketball floor. True to form, he made several of them, quipping, "I bet you Wilt Chamberlain can't do that."

Ali had a remarkable ability to connect with people. After his impromptu basketball display, he mingled with the crowd, signing autographs, kissing babies, and charming everyone around him. The larger-than-life champion was, at his core, a man who genuinely cared about others.

Later that year, during Thanksgiving week, I found myself in Cherry Hill, New Jersey, where Ali lived. My wife Diane, her aunt Wanda, and two cousins joined me in searching for his house. When we found it, Ali was up on the roof gathering leaves. I called out to him, and to my surprise, he invited us into his driveway. Ali, always the entertainer, came down from the roof and gave us a tour of his beautiful home. As we walked through the house, he even autographed photos for each of us.

It was in moments like these that the myth of the mean, cold-hearted boxing champion fell away, revealing the teddy bear he could be outside the ring.

Ali went on to reclaim his title by defeating the young champion George Foreman in the famous "Rumble in the Jungle" in Zaire. Everyone, even some of those in Ali's camp, thought Foreman would destroy him. But Ali, with his ingenious "rope-a-dope" strategy, wore out Foreman and proved the doubters wrong once again.

Ali's fame grew to unparalleled heights. He was recognized and adored worldwide, welcomed into the homes of movie stars and kings alike. Even Elvis Presley gifted him a custom-made boxing robe reportedly worth $5,000. Ali's charisma was such that when he spoke, everyone listened.

I was there in the New Orleans Superdome on September 15, 1978, when Ali regained his title for the third time, defeating Leon Spinks in front of 63,350 fans. Though Ali won that night, it was clear that his skills had diminished. I knew then that the end of his career was near. He fought twice more, losing both bouts—first to Larry Holmes in October 1980, where he was stopped in the 10th round, and then to Trevor Berbick in December 1981, where he lost a 10-round unanimous decision. These last fights, where Ali took a lot of punishment, were particularly hard on his body.

After retiring, Ali suffered from Parkinson's disease, a neurological disorder believed to have been caused by the repeated blows to the head he endured late in his career. The young Ali had been almost untouchable, but as he aged, the "rope-a-dope" style took its toll.

Despite the ravages of disease, Ali remained a beloved figure, a hero who transcended the sport of boxing. His impact was felt not just in the ring but around the world. He stood up for what he believed in, giving a voice to those who had none, and earned a place in history as one of the most influential figures of the 20th century.

Ali passed away on June 3, 2016, at the age of 74, leaving behind a legacy that will endure for generations.

— 8 —

Jimmy Heair: All He Has Left Is Courage

In 1981, at the age of 32, I moved to Memphis, Tennessee, to open and manage a new health club for a company based in Nashville. My routine involved commuting from Nashville to Memphis during the week and returning home on weekends. While in Memphis, I decided to reignite an old passion and began training as a boxer again at the Parks and Recreation boxing gym located at the fairgrounds.

At the gym, I connected with Jimmy Heair, a professional boxer who had once been ranked among the top 10 lightweights in the world during the mid-1970s. Heair had been good enough to go ten rounds with great world champions Nicolino Locche and Roberto Duran in non-title fights. Despite having over 100 professional bouts under his belt, Heair's skills had diminished, and he had moved up to fighting as a welterweight at the age of 30.

On my first day of training at the gym, Heair asked if I would spar with him. It had been about seven years since I had last sparred with a professional, and I was in terrible shape, so I couldn't give him much of a challenge. I would manage to go two or three rounds before running out of gas and needing to step out of the ring.

Still, I showed up at the gym every day, putting on my hand wraps, shorts, headgear, and boxing gloves, ready to work several rounds with Heair. He preferred using fighting gloves, which were only 8 ounces, rather than the 16-ounce training gloves typically used for sparring. Looking back, I realize how reckless that was—it's much easier to hurt someone with those smaller gloves.

Despite the intensity, I returned day after day, gradually getting in better shape. It took about three months before I could hold my own in the ring. I started at around 190 pounds and eventually dropped to 168 pounds. After three months, I was in such good condition that I could run nine miles, and sparring with Heair became easy. I even started seriously considering turning professional at the age of 32.

Heair had been on a winning streak, with 17 consecutive victories while fighting in Memphis. Former World Boxing Association heavyweight champion Ernie Terrell, who was promoting boxing in Chicago, reached out to Heair, offering him a fight against a welterweight named Roosevelt Green. Heair accepted the offer and asked me to accompany him to Chicago and work his corner during the fight.

I grew up just 50 miles north of Chicago and remembered seeing Green as an amateur. "I'll go with you and get a bunch of my friends from Wisconsin to come down and watch you fight," I told him.

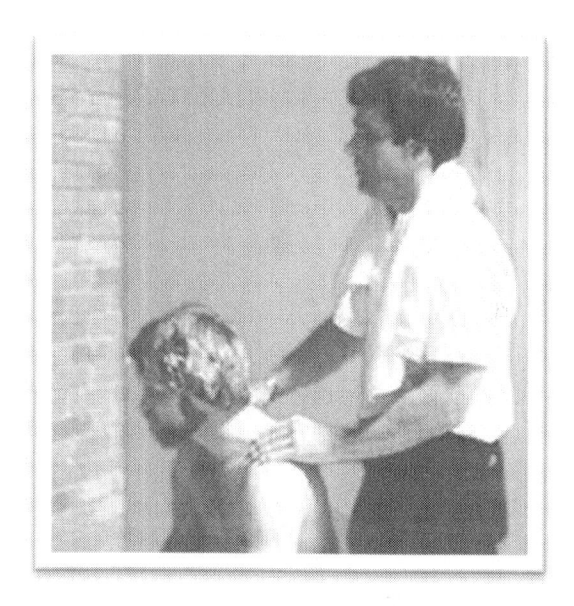

Jimmy Heair and Kerry Pharr waiting in the wings (1981)

We drove from Memphis to Chicago, making a stop in Kenosha, Wisconsin, where we stayed with my cousin Phil for a couple of days before the fight. While we were there, Heair wanted to get in one last day of sparring. We both gloved up and began sparring. Afterward, my friend and mentor Larry Freeman turned to me and said, "Kerry, you're too much of a man for him. You should go ahead and turn pro yourself." It was flattering to hear such praise from the man who had introduced me to boxing, but deep down, I knew my time in the ring had passed. The next day, we drove to Chicago, checked into our hotel on Lakeshore Drive, and rested up before the weigh-in the following day.

At the weigh-in, Roosevelt Green showed up, but he was ill and couldn't fight. Terrell quickly scrambled and found another opponent for Heair—a fighter from Indiana named Charlie Peterson. On May 4, 1981, Heair easily won a 10-round decision against Peterson, an ordinary fighter. Terrell then booked Heair and Green for a rescheduled match on June 29.

Heair managed his own career, often taking fights on short notice without giving his body enough time to recuperate between bouts. After leaving Chicago, he fought another match just eight days later in Memphis, scoring a second-round knockout against Tony Jordan. Three weeks later, on June 6, he won a 10-round unanimous decision against Don Morgan in Tupelo, Mississippi. However, when he finally faced Roosevelt Green on June 29 in Chicago, he lost a 10-round decision.

Around this time, I left Memphis and returned to Nashville, abandoning any thoughts of pursuing a professional boxing career. However, six months later, I was back in Memphis with Heair when he fought Bill "Fireball" Bradley in a 10-round main event at the Cook Convention Center.

**Roosevelt Green vs. Jimmy Heair
Chicago (June 1981)**

That night, we shared a dressing room with Irish Billy Collins Jr. of Nashville, who was fighting in his second professional bout. Collins Jr. was a promising young fighter, following in the footsteps of his father, Billy Sr., who had been a welterweight contender in the late 1950s and early 1960s. Billy Sr. had fought against future welterweight world champion Curtis Cokes for the Southern welterweight championship, losing on a 10-round decision. Earlier in his career, Billy Sr. had also handed "Irish" Bobby Cassidy his first professional loss, with Cassidy later becoming a top light-heavyweight contender.

I had met Cassidy when Dave Wolf brought him with former light heavyweight champion Donnie Lalonde to train at my gym. He told me, "I was just a kid when I fought Billy Collins, and he was already a tough veteran. When I walked past his dressing room the night of the fight and looked in, he was sound asleep. That really scared me."

Now, Collins' son was making his mark, scoring a second-round knockout against Gary Baker on January 19, 1982.

As for Heair, he lost his fight that night in a decision, and it was clear he was starting to look shopworn. Boxing commissions were established to regulate the sport and, most importantly, to protect the fighters. Those whose skills have diminished should not be allowed to continue fighting. This experience highlighted to me why boxing commissions are so crucial—they exist to protect fighters who may not know when to quit.

It's evident to everyone but the fighter when they become a shadow of their former selves—a "shot fighter," as they say. Boxers should retire long before they reach that point, but the allure of the spotlight, the fame, and the glory is like a drug, making it incredibly difficult to walk away. I witnessed this firsthand with Jimmy Heair on the night he lost the first fight of his career in which he wasn't competetive. I heard someone at ringside say, "All he has left is courage." They could see his skills had faded, and sadly, I saw it too.

After the fight, Heair began sobbing in the dressing room. "I hate to quit boxing. It's the only thing that made my life special. It's the only thing that separated me from the guy digging a ditch," he said.

I never worked his corner again because I couldn't bear to see what was happening to him. Many friends, both in and out of boxing, urged him to retire, but Heair continued fighting for several more years, likely only stopping when he could no longer get a license. Years later I was offered a position on the State of Tennessee's Boxing Advisory Board. I gladly served on the board from 1995 until my first wife passed away in October 2001. Shortly thereafter I walked away from the sport that I loved so much.

— 9 —

The Most Notorious Fight of All: Luis Resto vs. Billy Collins

On January 19, 1982, in Memphis, Tennessee, I first encountered the young and promising boxer, Irish Billy Ray Collins. I was in the dressing room with and worked the corner of Jimmy Heair who was headlining the 10-round main event that night, and we shared a dressing room with Collins. He was just starting his professional career, having already enjoyed a successful amateur run. With his father, Billy Sr., a renowned welterweight boxer from the 1960s, guiding him as both his manager and trainer, the younger Collins had boxing in his blood. That night, Collins secured a second-round knockout victory over Gary Baker in what was only his second professional fight. His striking good looks and raw talent marked him as a future star.

Since Collins hailed from the Nashville area, where I also lived, I followed his career closely. I introduced Billy and his father to Randy Weiler, a friend of mine who was a sportswriter for *The Nashville Banner*. Randy quickly recognized Collins' potential and wrote several articles highlighting his rising career. With an undefeated record and his father's influence, Collins caught the attention of Bob Arum's Top Rank Inc., the premier promotional company in boxing. All his fights would now be showcased on ESPN, and it seemed inevitable that Collins was on a path to stardom and a world championship title.

**Kerry Pharr, Keith McKnight,
Shayne Lavender, Billy Collins Sr.,
and Ken Atkin**

By 1983, with an impeccable 14-0 record, Top Rank decided to feature Collins in a nationally televised bout at Madison Square Garden. He was slated to fight on the undercard of the legendary Roberto

Duran, who was battling Davey Moore for the WBA light middleweight world championship. On June 16, 1983, before a roaring crowd of over 20,000 fans, Collins stepped into the ring as the heavy favorite against the relatively unknown journeyman, Luis Resto.

From the opening bell, something was wrong. Despite Collins' superior skill, Resto relentlessly battered him, leaving Collins' eyes grotesquely swollen. With each passing round, the beating intensified, far beyond what one would expect in a standard match. Billy Sr., sensing something was terribly amiss, approached Resto's corner after the final bell to shake hands—a customary gesture, but one that would reveal a horrifying truth. The moment Billy Sr. touched Resto's gloves, he realized there was little to no padding inside. He erupted, screaming at officials and the press, "There's no padding in these damn gloves!"

Chaos ensued as Resto's gloves were confiscated by the New York State Athletic Commission. An investigation revealed that Resto's trainer, Panama Lewis, had used tweezers to meticulously remove the horsehair padding from the gloves in the dressing room before the fight. This tampering had gone unnoticed by both the Collins' camp and the Commission.

Despite Resto's victory by unanimous decision, the fight was later ruled a no-contest. Resto and

Lewis were arrested in January of 1995, tried, and convicted of conspiracy to fix a fight, among other charges. Lewis was sentenced to a year in prison and banned for life from boxing in the United States. Resto served two and a half years in prison and was also banned from the sport. Collins' record was restored to 14-0, but the damage was irreversible. The crime was so horrendous that even HBO produced a documentary titled *Assault in the Ring*. The film is now available on YouTube.

The fight left Collins with permanent eye damage, and he was informed that he would never be able to box again. Stripped of his dream, he spiraled into depression. On the night of March 7, 1984, just nine months after the infamous fight, Collins was at a Nashville bar with his father and a friend, John Duke. After a night of drinking, his father took his car keys and handed them to Duke, asking him to drive Collins home. But outside the bar, Collins convinced Duke to return the keys.

Minutes later, at around 1 a.m., Collins was driving his Oldsmobile west on Old Franklin Road in Nashville when the car veered off an embankment into a creek, landing upside down. Collins was killed instantly. He was just 23 years old. Duke walked away with minor injuries, but the loss of Billy Collins was a devastating blow to everyone who knew him.

Billy Collins had been a rising star in the boxing world, his future seemingly limitless. Yet, in one night, his dreams were stolen, leading to a tragic and untimely end.

— 10 —

Darrell "Fast Fists" Fuller

After Jimmy Heair introduced me to the world of professional boxing management, I began training and managing the careers of other fighters.

Darryl "Fast Fists" Fuller was a world-class junior welterweight boxer whom I had the privilege of co-training and managing. In March 1985, Don King's Matchmaker, Payton Sher, helped me secure Fuller a shot at the World Boxing Council's Continental of Americas junior welterweight championship.

The reigning champion, Kel "Special K" Robin, was a formidable opponent. Standing six feet tall—an impressive height for a 140-pound fighter—Robin was an excellent boxer-puncher from Miami. Marty Cohen, the president of the WBC's Continental of America's Championship Committee, was helping to develop Robin, who was promoted by Don King Productions. To secure the fight for Fuller, we had to sign a promotional agreement with the legendary

Don King himself. With only six weeks to prepare, Darryl trained harder than ever.

Darryl was a seasoned veteran with an outstanding amateur background. Standing 5'7" with a powerful, muscular build, he was a relentless and fearless fighter. His aggressive style was all about constant pressure. He would close the distance, unleash a flurry of punches, and force his opponents into a fight they couldn't escape. His approach never allowed them a moment's rest.

**Rev. Leroy Ozier, Darryl Fuller, Kerry Pharr
Sands Hotel, Atlantic City (1985)**

One of Darryl's most unnerving habits was his grunting or barking with each punch he threw. This constant pressure often wore down his opponents both physically and emotionally. Darryl would often talk about how long it would take to break another fighter down or how many rounds he needed to take his opponent's heart. His fights were wars of attrition, and he usually succeeded in wearing his opponents down over several grueling rounds.

Darryl was all business in the ring, whether sparring at the gym or in a fight. He was just as vicious in training sessions as he was in actual bouts. Asking him to take it easy on an inexperienced boxer was out of the question—his style was too punishing. Anyone who stepped into the ring with him had to be ready for a real fight, or they had no business being there.

Outside the ring, Darryl and I shared many experiences together. Having spent little time in the countryside, he was fascinated by rural life, so I often took him and other fighters to places like the mountains or state parks. We visited Rideout Falls in Alabama and Fall Creek Falls State Resort Park in Tennessee, home to the highest waterfall in the U.S. east of the Mississippi River.

One of the funniest memories I have of Darryl was during one of our rural trips when we spotted a possum in the middle of the road. Darryl, with a grin, started shouting, "Run over that possum, Kerry!" I laughed and refused, saying, "You're crazy; I'm not running over that possum." But Darryl persisted, "Yeah, run over it!" I kept driving without hitting it, and Darryl looked at me with disappointment, saying, "Man, that's the best tasting sandwich meat there is—especially with some hot sauce."

The fight with Robin took place at the Las Vegas Riviera Hotel. As we entered the ring, I noticed comedian and TV star Redd Foxx sitting ringside in our corner, chatting with former welterweight world champion Hedgeman Lewis. But my focus was entirely on Fuller as the ring announcer introduced him and the reigning champion, Robin.

After the introductions, referee Davey Pearl called us to the center of the ring for final instructions. We returned to our corner, and I helped Fuller remove his robe while his co-trainer, Rev. Leroy Ozier, quickly inserted his mouthpiece. The timekeeper rang the bell, and the fight began.

Uncharacteristically, Fuller walked straight at his much taller opponent with his left hand down. Robin seized the moment, throwing a perfectly timed, fast and hard right hand that landed flush on Fuller's chin. Darryl went down towards the end of the first round, like a tree limb hitting the ground after a storm.

Bobby Goodman, vice president of boxing for Don King Productions, later told me he thought Fuller was about to get blown out in the first round, potentially ruining the televised event. Everyone in the arena thought the fight was over and that Robin had already won.

But Fuller calmly rose to his feet at the count of eight, glanced at Rev. Ozier and me in his corner, and nodded as if to say, "I'm OK, and I know what to do." The referee wiped Darryl's gloves and motioned for the fight to continue.

In preparation for this bout, we had traveled to Morristown, Tennessee, where Darryl sparred with future world champion Frankie "The Surgeon" Randall. Randall would later become the first fighter to dethrone the legendary junior welterweight champion Julio Cesar Chavez. Fuller and Randall pushed each other to the limit, trading wins in their sparring sessions. This rigorous training had prepared Fuller well for anything Robin could throw at him.

Robin tried to crush Fuller, but he couldn't land another clean shot or discourage Darryl. As Darryl returned to the corner at the end of the first round, Rev. Ozier and I tried to keep him calm, reassuring him that he could still win.

From the second round on, Fuller began to impose his will on Robin. He drew the champion into a brawl, roughing him up and slowly breaking him down. The war of attrition and the battle of wills played out over the next seven brutal rounds, with both fighters trading heavy blows like two rock-em, sock-em robots. I could see Robin slowly unraveling.

By the ninth round, the constant pressure Fuller applied finally broke Robin down physically and emotionally. Fuller knocked Robin down in the ninth round, again in the 10th, and twice more in the 11th. Fortunately, Davey Pearl stepped in and stopped the fight before Fuller could inflict any more damage. Fuller won the bout and the championship via a technical knockout in the 11th round.

While I was thrilled that my fighter had won, I couldn't help but feel sorry for Kel Robin, who left the ring a broken man. I never heard of him again after that night. Darryl Fuller had effectively ended his career on March 15, 1985. Fuller became a champion because he had the strength and courage to get up after that first-round knockdown and fight his way back to victory.

Fast Fists Sits on Ice

Unfortunately, after Fast Fists Fuller won the Continental championship, our promoter Don King put him on ice, never giving him another fight. Darrell, being a full-time professional fighter, couldn't make a living without getting in the ring. Several years later, I became a boxing promoter, organizing numerous shows each year to keep my fighters active while building their records and waiting for a big-money opportunity. But at that time, I was just a boxing manager with no experience in promoting, which made it incredibly difficult to secure fights for Fuller.

The junior welterweight division was particularly competitive then, with the great Aaron Pryor holding one of the titles and Gene "Mad Dog" Hatcher holding another. Just two weeks before Fuller won the Continental title, Aaron Pryor narrowly escaped losing his world championship to Gary Hinton, a tall, slick southpaw boxer from Philadelphia. Hinton was outboxing Pryor and was on the verge of taking his title, but Pryor in desperation managed to knock Hinton down in the 14th round, scraping by with a narrow split-decision victory.

Fuller Inactive While Stablemate Bowers Fights Sumbu Kalambay

That summer, I managed to secure a tune-up fight for Fuller, but it wasn't enough to help him cover his bills. In July, I booked a dream match for Donald Bowers, one of Darrell Fuller's stablemates, in the picturesque and opulent city of Monte Carlo. The opponent? Sumbu Kalambay, a future world champion from the Congo fighting under the banner of the legendary Italian promoter Rodolfo Sabatini. Bowers and Kalambay had crossed paths years earlier in an international amateur fight, where Bowers had claimed victory. But this time, in Monte Carlo, the stakes were higher.

Donald was a disciplined athlete, training rigorously every day, and when he was in peak condition, he could run five miles in 30 minutes without breaking a sweat. His talent and hard work, combined with the guidance of his exceptional amateur coach,

Rayford Collins, helped him win two national championships and build an impressive 21-3 professional record. But discipline in the ring didn't always translate to discipline outside it. Like many of us, Donald had his struggles, particularly with food. Bowers had trained with Rayford Collins for the fight in his hometown of Jackson, Tennessee. By the time we arrived in France for the Kalambay fight, he was 15 pounds over his contracted weight. He admitted to me that once he started eating, he couldn't stop until he was full—a common struggle for many, but one that had serious consequences for a professional fighter.

Bowers managed to cut weight in the week leading up to the fight, but it left him weak, and Kalambay, soon to be the middleweight world champion, took full advantage.

Despite putting up a valiant effort, Bowers lost the bout in a unanimous decision, marking Kalambay's rise while reminding us of the cruel and unforgiving nature of the sport.

— 11 —

Hall of Fame Matchmaker Teddy Brenner

When we returned to the States, I stayed behind in New York City with a mission: to meet with Teddy Brenner, the no-nonsense matchmaker for Bob Arum's Top Rank Inc. I was eager to pitch Darrell Fuller for a shot at Junior Welterweight Champion Gene Hatcher. After some persistence, Brenner finally let me into his Manhattan office. He was as blunt as his reputation suggested. When I laid out Fuller's credentials, Brenner responded with a stinging reality check.

"I want you to go downstairs, stand on the sidewalk, and start yelling Darrell Fuller's name," he said. "See how many people in New York know who he is." His words hit hard. He wasn't just dismissing Fuller; he was dismissing the marketability of my fighter. To Brenner, Fuller was just another tough contender, but not one who could fill seats or generate buzz. My heart sank, knowing Fuller's talent alone wasn't enough to get him the shot he deserved.

Brenner Takes Call from Mike Tyson's Manager, Cus D'Amato

While I was sitting in Brenner's office, the phone rang at his secretary's desk. She called out, "Teddy, Gregorio Benitez—Wilfred Benitez's father—is on the line and wants to talk to you." Without missing a beat, Brenner shouted back, "Tell him to lose my number!"

After a brief pause, though, Brenner reconsidered and decided to take Gregorio's call. At this point, the great champion Wilfred's best days as a boxer were behind him, and Brenner probably figured that Benitez was "shot" as a fighter. Still, he picked up the phone and listened to what Gregorio had to say. Gregorio was doing exactly what I had been trying to do—pitching his fighter for a big-money bout, insisting that his son was back on track after a recent win. Brenner exchanged a few polite words with him before abruptly ending the conversation.

Almost as soon as he hung up, the secretary called out again, "Teddy, Cus D'Amato is on the phone." D'Amato, the legendary trainer who had developed champions like Floyd Patterson and José Torres, was now guiding a young heavyweight prospect named Mike Tyson, who was gearing up for his first six-round fight.

Brenner took the call, and I could hear D'Amato expressing some doubt, saying he wasn't sure Tyson could go six rounds. Brenner quickly reassured him, "The kid I've got Tyson fighting can't go six rounds. We're going to make your fighter the heavyweight 'cham-peen' of the world."

After a few more words, Brenner hung up the phone. I thanked him for his time, shook his hand, and said goodbye, knowing I'd just witnessed a small but fascinating glimpse into the world of boxing's biggest players.

— 12 —

"Fast Fists" Fuller Defends Title Against Gary Hinton

At the end of the summer, I received a call from the renowned Philadelphia boxing promoter, Russell Peltz. He made an offer for Darrell Fuller to fight against his fighter, Gary Hinton—the same Gary Hinton who had nearly upset Aaron Pryor for the world championship just two weeks before Darrell won the Continental title that March. I was hesitant, to say the least. Hinton was a tall, six-foot southpaw, tough as nails, and an exceptionally slick boxer. After seeing how close he came to defeating the great Aaron Pryor, I didn't see a clear path to victory for us.

However, the reality was that we had to defend the title or risk losing it by default, and Darrell was eager—desperate, even—for the fight with Hinton. So, on November 5, 1985, Darrell Fuller faced Gary Hinton at the Sands Hotel and Casino in Atlantic City, New Jersey. It turned out to be a 12-round war.

During the fight, Fast Fists managed to cut Hinton above his right eye and bust his nose, but when the final bell rang, Hinton was awarded a unanimous decision. He won the fight fair and square, and Darrell was never quite the same afterward.

My contract with Darrell expired, and he eventually moved to New York, where Al Certo took over his training. Darrell became a sparring partner for world champion Buddy McGirt, marking a significant shift in his career losing two out of three of his next fights by knockout. Meanwhile, Gary Hinton won the world championship in his next bout.

— 13 —

The Murder of Donald Bowers

Donald "Battling" Bowers was grappling with his own problems and addictions. During the build-up to the fight, Bowers and I had a candid conversation about the dangers of addiction, specifically cocaine. In his straightforward way, he said, "Once is too many, and a thousand times is never enough."

After his loss to Kalambay, Donald retired from boxing for two years. In 1987, he approached me, asking for help to stage a comeback. I managed to get him some sparring sessions with future world champion Darrin Van Horn, along with a couple of victories on the undercard of Van Horn's main events. In July, I matched him against an average fighter, Franklin Owens, in Memphis, Tennessee, but he lost a six-round split decision.

A few days later, Philadelphia promoter Russell Peltz called, offering Bowers one last chance to revive his career with a fight against Robert "Bam Bam" Hines, another slick southpaw from

Philadelphia who would soon become a world champion. The bout was scheduled for August 18th, just five weeks after his loss in Memphis.

Donald Bowers brings his "Rocky" impersonation to the Philadelphia landmark made famous by actor Sylvester Stallone

The first round of the fight was competitive, and the beginning of the second showed promise. But as

Bowers tried to maneuver away from Hines, he was struck by a straight left hand, causing him to stumble and become entangled in the ropes. His left arm was wrapped around the top rope, and his right arm was caught in the bottom rope. Trapped like a fly in a spider web, he was unable to defend himself. Hines continued to land punches on the helpless Bowers until referee Rudy Battle intervened, stopping the fight and declaring Hines the winner by TKO. Though the fight was later ruled a no-contest, the damage was done, and Bowers' boxing career came to an end.

I had always gotten along with Bowers, and I genuinely cared for him. I had never seen him use drugs or harm anyone else. However, on June 16th, 1989, two years after his boxing career ended, he was arrested for aggravated assault. Over the next two decades, he was arrested fourteen more times.

In 2011, police officers pulled him over for weaving along the highway while driving. According to the report, Bowers struggled with the officers outside his car after attempting to swallow a gram of crack cocaine wrapped in plastic. After being sprayed twice in the face with "Freeze" spray, he finally spit out the bag of drugs. The officers also found ten 7.5 mg Hydrocodone pills wrapped in a napkin in his front pants pocket.

Donald's life took a tragic turn on May 16, 2012, when he was found dead in his home in Jackson,

Tennessee, marking the city's fifth homicide that year. His death created a deep void in the community, especially at the Jackson Boxing Club, where he had taken over as coach in 2009. Despite his struggles with crime and the law, Donald was highly regarded in Jackson, Tennessee. "He was a father figure and a mentor," said Obie Beard, a former teammate. "He was great with the kids, training them every day and making sure they had money for trips."

In the ring, Donald defied expectations, securing a third-place finish in the Olympic trials despite doubts about his size. However, his greatest legacy, according to those who knew and loved him, was the impact he had on the youth he mentored. Many of these young people saw him as the only father figure they ever had.

Within the boxing community, Donald is remembered not just for his accomplishments in the ring, but for the lives he touched while training young boxers. His legacy lives on in the hearts of those he guided. Bowers' murder remains unsolved, serving as a stark reminder of the struggles and dangers that exist outside the ring.

— 14 —

Diamond Jim MacDonald

We had just landed in Johannesburg, South Africa, after a long and tiring flight. I was with Diamond Jim MacDonald, a professional boxer scheduled to fight Thulane "Sugar Boy" Malinga in the main event of a boxing show. MacDonald and I had left the United States two days before, flying from Kennedy International Airport in New York to London's Heathrow International Airport, where we had a 14-hour layover.

Besides being a light-heavyweight contender, MacDonald was an avid antique collector and dealer. We landed in London just after daybreak and, with plenty of time before our evening departure to South Africa, we decided to take the train downtown. After getting off at Piccadilly Circus, we had breakfast and spent the day exploring antique shops along the Thames River. Near the end of the day, MacDonald found an antique bottle that had been fished out of the Thames, which he purchased before we headed back to Heathrow for our evening flight.

We were flying South African Airlines during the days of Apartheid, a system of racial separation. The airline had a strict policy of searching every passenger and their baggage before boarding, which slowed down the process significantly. Due to international boycotts against the white-ruled South African government, South African Airlines wasn't allowed to fly the shortest route down the continent of Africa. Instead, we took a longer route around the Ivory Coast, stopping on a small island west of the coast to refuel before continuing to Johannesburg.

After arriving in Johannesburg, we were greeted by the show's promoters, South African Thinus Strydom and Ireland native Jim Harvey, who welcomed us and made us feel comfortable. We collected our baggage and were driven to our hotel in Johannesburg, or Jo-burg as the locals call it.

MacDonald was originally from Flint, Michigan, and had developed as a boxer while serving in the United States Marine Corps. After being discharged, he trained at Emanuel Steward's famed Kronk Gym in Detroit before turning professional in Phoenix, Arizona. He later moved to Ft. Payne, Alabama, to train with former Marine boxing teammate Lane Killien, who introduced him to prominent Nashville attorney Stan Allen. Allen, a capable manager and promoter, worked closely with Bob Arum of Top Rank, Inc., and managed MacDonald as well as other notable boxers. MacDonald and his wife, Traci, moved to Nashville to further his career.

MacDonald wasn't the most skillful boxer, but he had a powerful right hand that could knock out a mule. He would wait for his opponent to jab, then rock back on his right foot and counter with that huge right hand. If it connected, the fight usually ended.

Allen put MacDonald on his boxing shows, and Jim started knocking out fighters left and right. Despite his success, he wasn't rated due to his lack of amateur credentials, and the national media didn't take notice. However, Allen secured a fight for MacDonald against Willie Edwards, the number one-rated light-heavyweight boxer in the world. MacDonald had sparred with Edwards while training at Kronk and was confident he could win the bout.

The fight took place in Houston, Texas, on February 17, 1985. In the fourth round, MacDonald caught Edwards with his big right hand, knocking him out and securing a top-10 world ranking. This earned him a title fight against the great light-heavyweight champion Michael Spinks.

On June 6, 1985, MacDonald faced Spinks at the Las Vegas Riviera Hotel. Although MacDonald managed to hurt Spinks with his right hand, Spinks never went down and ultimately stopped MacDonald via a technical knockout in the eighth round.

Jim MacDonald, Michael Spinks, former light-heavyweight and heavyweight world champion, and Kerry Pharr

While in Nashville, MacDonald and I became friends. I owned a health club there and managed junior welterweight Continental of America's champion Darryl "Fast Fists" Fuller. Even though Fuller was much smaller, he and Jim were frequent sparring partners. After MacDonald's fight with Spinks and the end of his contract with Allen, I briefly promoted MacDonald in 1988 and '89.

After resting for a few hours at our hotel in Johannesburg, Jim Harvey came by as he called it, to collect us for a South African barbecue at a country club. Strydom informed us that the South African television media wanted footage of MacDonald boxing, so we were scheduled to go to a gym in Jo-burg the next day.

At the gym, the television reporters and print media were present. They introduced us to the boxer who was supposed to spar with MacDonald. However, I didn't feel comfortable with him sparring someone we didn't know, especially with three weeks left before the bout. I didn't want to risk MacDonald getting injured, so I volunteered to spar with him instead. We worked a couple of light rounds, and the television crew got their footage for the evening news.

Throughout our time in South Africa, Strydom and Harvey treated us like royalty, but I knew they were promoting Malinga, and we were the supporting cast. The national media treated us like VIPs, constantly seeking our opinions and organizing press conferences to help promote the upcoming show.

To generate interest in the fight, we were taken everywhere to hype the bout. At one press conference, Malinga's promoter, Jim Harvey, whispered in my ear, encouraging me to push Malinga into a swimming pool to create excitement. However, I had grown to respect Malinga, a humble and decent man born into poverty in a Zulu village. I decided not to push him into the pool, as I didn't want to insult him.

While in South Africa, we visited hostels where Xhosa, Zulu, and Swazi tribesmen who worked in the gold mines lived. We also went to soccer fields where the boxers were introduced to large crowds. Before leaving the U.S., I had packed a gym bag with

Gideon New Testaments to give away. At one soccer field, Jim Harvey announced that I had Bibles to distribute, and the tribesmen rushed to me, eager to receive them. I was touched by how receptive the South Africans were to the Gospel of Jesus Christ, particularly the Black South Africans I met. Many eagerly prayed with me to accept Christ as their savior.

The South African media made a star out of Diamond Jim in the short time we were there. The boxing match was held in Klerksdorp, South Africa, at Oppenheimer Stadium, and we left Johannesburg for Klerksdorp two weeks before the fight.

At our hotel in Klerksdorp, a beautiful young woman who worked there became infatuated with Diamond Jim. Despite being far from home and the temptation she presented, MacDonald remained faithful to his wife and his Christian values, repeatedly turning her down.

The night of the fight, March 7, 1988, Oppenheimer Stadium was filled with fans eager to see Malinga and MacDonald in the 10-round main event. Although MacDonald was in good shape, he struggled with the high altitude in South Africa and appeared sluggish during the bout. He knocked Malinga down in the seventh round with a powerful right hand, but Malinga got up and outworked MacDonald, earning a unanimous decision.

Several years later, Malinga traveled to England

and upset Nigel Benn to win the World Boxing Council super-middleweight world championship. He returned home to a hero's welcome, with Nelson Mandela pinning the championship belt around his waist.

Sadly, my dear friend Diamond Jim passed away on August 19, 2023, from the same ailments that claimed the great Muhammad Ali: Parkinson's and Alzheimer's disease. Boxing is a brutal sport, and many fighters endure lasting physical consequences from the relentless training and grueling battles they face in the ring.

— 15 —

Tim Johnson vs. David Bates: Dueling Head Butts

On May 5, 1992, my boxer, Tim "Scrap Iron" Johnson, was squaring off against David Bates, a rugged and unorthodox fighter from Odessa, Texas. This was the main event at the New Daisy Theatre on Beale Street in Memphis, Tennessee. During the bout, Bates accidentally caught Johnson with a head butt. When Johnson returned to our corner between rounds, he was fuming.

"Kerry, he just hit me with a head butt," Johnson vented.

"It was probably an accident, but be careful and don't get cut," I advised.

"I'm going to get him back," Johnson shot back with determination.

As soon as the bell rang for the next round, Johnson charged across the ring like a bull, smashing his head into Bates' forehead with all his might. The impact was so forceful that it opened a massive gash on Johnson's own head. After the fight, instead of celebrating, Johnson and I spent the night in a hospital emergency room as doctors stapled his skull to close the wound he had inflicted on himself.

This incident was just one of many in the tumultuous life of Timmy Johnson. His parents had abandoned him in a laundromat when he was a child, leading him to grow up as an orphan at the Tennessee Baptist Children's Home. At age 13, he was adopted by Tommy and Pat Johnson, a wonderful Christian couple who already had three biological children but were dedicated to caring for other children in need. Timmy was their first adopted child, and he proudly took on the family name.

I started teaching Johnson how to box when he was 18. He was a strikingly handsome young man with an undeniable charisma. I recall one evening when we were having dinner before an amateur boxing tournament in Knoxville, Tennessee. A waitress approached our table and asked him, "Do you have a girlfriend?" Before he could respond, she added, "Would you like one?"

Despite his outward charm, Johnson had endured a difficult childhood before meeting his adoptive parents, and the trauma was evident in his behavior. He could be incredibly kind one moment, and then, in a flash, something would trigger a rage within him. Though managing him was often challenging, I grew to love the kid and his family deeply. He reminded me so much of myself when I was younger—wounded, angry, bitter, and carrying a massive chip on his shoulder. He could easily have been mistaken for my cousin Timmy Pharr's twin.

Johnson was a tough, cocky brawler, earning him the nickname "Scrap Iron." We also called him T.J. He loved verbal confrontations almost as much as physical ones, emulating Muhammad Ali by engaging in trash talk with his opponents and anyone else who dared to spar with him verbally.

"Geez, Timmy, I Didn't Mean for You to Kill Him"

T.J. wasn't known for his knockout power, but I remember one incident during his amateur career when he hurt another boxer—and it was entirely my fault.

Our original boxing team was dubbed "Club Knockout" by a local newspaper reporter, and the name stuck. Johnson, Ken "The Bull" Atkin, and "Dangerous" Don Wilford were the founding members of the team. For over a decade we trained in a small cinderblock building that the mayor of La Vergne, Tennessee, had allowed us to use as a gym. The building's upstairs area, with its carpeted wooden floor, served as our makeshift boxing ring, roped off for sparring sessions. We had about twenty young men learning the art of boxing in that small space.

Among them was a tall, rugged fellow named Lonnie, about 21 years old, who had a hard time following instructions. Each time I let him spar, he tried to annihilate his partner. In the gym, I had a strict rule against one boxer abusing another. Sure, someone might get clipped on the chin and knocked down or even out, but that was rare. The boxers always wore protective gear, including 16-ounce training gloves, headgear, a protective cup, and a mouthpiece. We were careful to keep things under control during practice.

At the time, I was a relatively young coach and didn't handle the situation with Lonnie very well. I was trying to teach him and the other guys how to box, which usually involved weeks of technique work on the heavy bag, double-end bag, and speed bag before I allowed them to start "controlled sparring." When sparring began, it was always between two boxers of similar age, weight, and skill level, and they were only permitted to use their jabs.

The jab is the most important punch a boxer learns. It's not the most powerful, but it's often the most effective. A good jab sets up all the other punches. For a right-handed boxer, the left jab is the lead, while the right hand, left hook, and uppercut are the power punches. Larry Holmes, the former world heavyweight champion, dominated the division for seven years largely because of his great left jab. He knew that to control an opponent, you had to establish the jab first. Teaching a boxer to throw a jab is the first lesson; mastering the other punches takes months or even years.

Lonnie was sparring with another boxer, who was dutifully using only his jab as instructed. But despite my repeated warnings, Lonnie threw wild right hands and screamed at his sparring partners, clearly trying to hurt them. I was frustrated and angry, and I knew I had to put someone more experienced in the ring with him.

Tim Johnson, Ken Atkin, and Don Wilford had been training for a couple of months longer than Lonnie. So, I decided to glove up Johnson, who was 19 at the time, and whispered in his ear, "I want you to teach this kid a lesson."

As soon as the bell rang, Lonnie let out a blood-curdling scream and charged across the ring toward Johnson. I think it startled Timmy, and out of fear, he unleashed an incredibly vicious right hand that landed squarely on Lonnie's mouth.

Lonnie crashed to the floor with such force that the building shook as if we were experiencing an earthquake. Johnson had knocked Lonnie out cold, and blood was pouring from his mouth where his tooth had punctured his lip. His face turned ghostly pale, and he looked seriously hurt. It was a terrifying moment for me, and I blurted out, "Geez, Timmy, I didn't mean for you to kill him!"

Jimmy Brindley, another boxer watching the sparring session, was so shaken by the knockout that he immediately took off his gloves, left the gym, and never returned.

He later told another boxer, "Man, he hit him so hard I saw the light. That's the end of my boxing career."

About fifteen or twenty seconds later, Lonnie regained consciousness. He needed a few stitches in his mouth, but other than his bruised pride, he was okay. However, he never returned to the boxing gym either.

As an amateur, Johnson went on to win the Mid-State Golden Gloves and several other regional tournaments. Early in his professional career, he had some excellent opportunities, even fighting for two world championships.

On June 15, 1992, just five weeks after the bout with Bates, Johnson faced the hard-hitting Randall Younker for the World Boxing Federation light-heavyweight world championship. Johnson was stopped in the fifth round but found more success in the lighter super-middleweight division.

In November 1993, Johnson and I traveled to Brazil, where he was set to face Luciana Torres for the WBF super-middleweight world championship the day before Thanksgiving. Johnson had a good chance of winning, but a clash of heads with Torres resulted in a cut that ultimately cost him the fight.

While in Brazil, the promoter took us around the large city of Recife for newspaper, radio, and television appearances to help promote the upcoming championship fight, as is customary in most promotions.

Tim Johnson – Luciano Torres

During a visit to a large open-air market, Johnson got into a heated exchange with some local Brazilian vendors. He said something that offended a local butcher, who emerged from behind his counter and began threatening us with a meat cleaver in front of a large, excited crowd. Johnson wisely toned down the rhetoric, and we managed to escape without injury.

Although it was November, we were south of the equator, and the weather in Brazil was hot and steamy. The fight was held in an open bullfight arena, and the atmosphere was intense.

Johnson boxed well against the Brazilian known as "Todo Duro," which translates to "Hard as Steel." Despite being cut in the second or third round, Johnson was outboxing Torres. However, his showboating and taunting of Torres infuriated the partisan crowd, who began throwing things into the ring. This only fueled Johnson's fire, and he grew bolder as the fight progressed.

Torres never seriously hurt Johnson, and the cut wasn't severe, but in the eighth round, the referee stepped in and stopped the fight. Johnson was extremely disappointed, believing he was close to winning a world championship.

After the fight, the same crowd that had been so angry with Johnson during the bout embraced him afterward, treating him like a rock star. For Johnson, who had experienced so little love as a child, this overwhelming adulation was both a blessing and a curse. He was starving for affection, but even the outpouring of love from this crowd wasn't enough to heal the deep-rooted pain he had carried since childhood.

— 16 —

Keith McKnight

In my 30s, I opened a boxing gym in Middle Tennessee, driven by my passion as a professional boxing manager, trainer, and promoter. One of my most promising prospects was Keith McKnight, a boxer I had been mentoring since his teenage years. Alongside managing fighters, I had also begun promoting professional boxing shows.

Keith was a tall, lanky 17-year-old when he walked into our gym in a Nashville, Tennessee, suburb. Standing at 6'6" and weighing just 165 pounds, he was impossible to miss. I asked, "Hey, kid, what are you doing here?"

"I want to box," he replied confidently.

I couldn't help but be skeptical. "You must be kidding. These guys will break you in half in that boxing ring."

But he wasn't joking. "No, I want to box," he insisted.

He was so thin he looked like the son of Olive

Oyl, Popeye's girlfriend from the vintage cartoons. I truly doubted he could handle the rigors of boxing. His first amateur bout in Evansville, Indiana, was shaky, as he faced a smaller, more experienced opponent. But despite my initial doubts, he quickly developed into a very good amateur boxer within his first year. Our amateur boxing team had been growing in success, earning us the nickname "Club Knockout" from a local sports reporter, a moniker the boxers embraced.

Kerry Pharr, HOF Champ Curtis Cokes, Warren Williams, Keith McKnight

The original team included fighters like Ken "The Bull" Atkin, "Dangerous" Don Wilford, and Tim "Scrap Iron" Johnson—grown men who, in the early days, often roughed up young Keith. But I saw something special in McKnight. I could see his world-class potential and knew that with time, he would outgrow and out-skill my other boxers.

Early in his development, his potential was as apparent. I believed we could transform him into a world champion. He went on to win the Mid-State Golden Gloves three years in a row, as well as the Spirit of America Championship two consecutive years. In 1991, he was voted Best Boxer and Boxer of the Year at the Spirit of America tournament.

In 1992, at the Southern Golden Gloves championship, Keith faced future Olympian and heavyweight title challenger Calvin Brock. That night, a talented but hesitant Keith McKnight lost the decision. Brock later told Keith that he "felt he had received the decision over a more talented boxer." After that loss, McKnight decided to turn professional, despite being green and inexperienced.

Keith was a naturally gifted athlete—tall, quick, mobile, with decent power. However, he struggled with self-confidence. I took him under my wing, nurturing and protecting him as if he were my own son. I was convinced we could mold him into a world champion.

"You've got to Knock Him Out to Win!"

As I mentioned earlier, Keith McKnight arrived

at our Middle Tennessee gym as a tall (6'6"), skinny (165 lbs.) 17-year-old. I introduced him to boxing and trained him for ten years, serving as his coach throughout his amateur days and later sharing those duties with other trainers during his pro career. As an amateur, Keith compiled a 32-7 record and won numerous regional tournaments, including the Golden Gloves. When he turned pro, he bulked up to 220 pounds.

Keith was a popular, good-natured young man with a penchant for practical jokes. He loved making people laugh and would often have a new joke to share every day. After growing up, he worked at a bar and grill owned by his future father-in-law. One of his favorite pranks involved a bottle of hot sauce made from some of the hottest peppers in the world. The sauce was so potent it could probably serve as paint remover and was nearly inedible. Keith would bet people they couldn't handle the sauce, and when they inevitably couldn't, their faces would turn beet red as they gagged and choked, desperately drinking anything in sight to douse the fire in their mouths. Keith would throw his head back and laugh heartily, saying, "I tried to tell you it was too hot to eat."

Keith would go on to become one of the most graceful boxers you'd ever see. He had tremendous God-given athletic ability—height, speed, great coordination, quick hands, and exceptional mobility. His only physical drawback was his slender build.

Critics said he didn't hit hard enough, lacked courage, and wasn't physically strong enough to compete as a top-tier heavyweight. And being a white heavyweight in a sport where "Great White Hopes" were rare since the days of Jack Johnson didn't make things easier.

Keith McKnight, Kerry Pharr, and Former Heavyweight Champ James "Bonecrusher" Smith

I remember watching Muhammad Ali on TV during his prime and thinking he looked thin. But when I saw Ali in person for the first time, I was struck by the thickness of his body. Joe Frazier and

Mike Tyson were shorter heavyweights, but their bodies were thick and muscular. In person, "Big" George Foreman looked as huge and round as a mighty oak tree. By pro football standards, Foreman was massive. Keith was taller than most heavyweights, including Foreman and Ali, but he lacked their thick torso.

George Foreman Refuses to Fight McKnight

Despite the critics, McKnight compiled an impressive pro record of 33 wins and only 1 defeat, with 22 of his victories coming by knockout. He was so quick and elusive that even George Foreman, the former heavyweight champion, refused to fight him.

In 1997, Foreman's promoter, Bob Arum of Top Rank Inc., had a fight lined up for Foreman on HBO. Sean Gibbons, one of Top Rank's matchmakers, called me and said, "We've got an HBO date for Big George in April. I need you to send some video of McKnight's fights for Foreman to look at. We might be able to get your guy a date on HBO with the champ."

This potential opportunity was exhilarating because a win against the legendary, former two-time world champion would have catapulted McKnight's career. A fight on HBO against Foreman could have earned McKnight over $200,000. I quickly compiled some highlights and sent the video the next day. But after reviewing the tape, Foreman turned down McKnight as his opponent, opting instead to fight the stronger, less mobile, power-punching Lou Savarese.

During a speaking engagement in Nashville, Foreman told Nashville Banner sportswriter Randy Weiler that he didn't want to face the skillful McKnight because he was too quick and elusive.

"I don't want to fight somebody I've got to chase around that ring," Foreman said. "Somebody's gonna get their jaw hurt fighting that boy."

In addition to being a great champion, Foreman had a wonderful sense of humor. When asked once whether he worried about brain damage, he quipped, "Not really. Anybody going into boxing already has brain damage." Maybe there was some truth to that, but George Foreman was one of the shrewdest businessmen in the history of the sport.

Keith McKnight's Greatest Triumph

Team McKnight had signed an agreement with one of boxing's premier promoters, Cedric Kushner. Kushner put McKnight in four televised bouts, and McKnight won all four. The first of these victories came in July 1996, when McKnight knocked out the rugged, power-punching Tui Toia of Samoa in the first round in Houston. In his next televised fight,

McKnight secured a 10-round unanimous decision against the tough Eddie Donaldson in Asbury Park, N.J., in May 1997. Then, in July, McKnight registered a quick, first-round knockout of big Brian Scott at the Nez Perce Indian Reservation in Lewiston, Idaho. The biggest fight of McKnight's career came next, against Phil Jackson in Nashville.

Keith McKnight never won a world title, never fought for one, and never had a million-dollar payday. Yet, he was a success in the sport of boxing. I have never been prouder of him than the night he faced and defeated the dangerous Phil Jackson, a former challenger for the world heavyweight title. To this day, I take pride in having guided McKnight into a position where he could face fighters of Jackson's caliber.

The day McKnight faced Jackson was one of the hardest days of my life. While training for the Jackson bout, my beloved wife of 28 years, Diane, was diagnosed with breast cancer. She had a mastectomy just a few days before the bout, and we brought her home from the hospital on October 2, 1997—the day of the McKnight-Jackson fight.

Diane's mother came to stay with us to help care for her, but despite her condition, Diane insisted that I be with Keith. She had watched him grow up and had come to love him. Her concern for Keith's well-being outweighed her own.

The fight venue, Municipal Auditorium, was

fortunately only 30 minutes from our home. My close friend, Rev. Ken Collins, accompanied me to the fight, trying to comfort me along the way. But the stress of my wife's illness was nearly unbearable, and I struggled to focus that night. I was worried not only about Diane but also about the danger McKnight might face from the power-punching Jackson.

In the dressing room, I wrapped Keith's hands with two rolls of gauze per hand, as was our custom. McKnight began warming up by shadowboxing, and after he broke a sweat, we applied Vaseline to his face and body to protect him from cuts. He donned his large leather protective cup, boxing trunks, and 10-ounce Mexican-manufactured Reyes boxing gloves, which I consider the world's finest. These gloves, known as a puncher's glove, conform tightly to a boxer's fist, making a punch feel almost like hitting with bare knuckles—a potential advantage for Jackson, who was a bona fide puncher. It was nearly time for the walk to the ring.

As we sat in the dressing room, waiting for the call to the ring, Jackson was preparing in the other dressing room. Phil Jackson had fought Lennox Lewis for the heavyweight world championship. He was no joke—a bad dude on a mission, and if you were in the other corner, he intended to hurt you. Many in the boxing world referred to Jackson as a killer. He hit with astounding power, capable of a one-punch knockout with either hand, and, like former heavyweight champion Mike Tyson, he fought with bad intentions.

During the second round of the fight, Jackson walked to the center of the ring and, with precision timing, threw a devastating right hand that caught McKnight square on the chin, sending him crashing to the canvas. Most fighters would have stayed down, letting the referee count them out after taking such a brutal shot. A fighter with no courage might have given up, but not McKnight. After being knocked down, he rolled over and steadied himself on one knee.

When the referee's count reached eight, McKnight rose to his feet and tried to shake the cobwebs from his head. After the referee wiped McKnight's gloves, he motioned for the fight to continue. Jackson, like a lion stalking its prey, swarmed McKnight. Faking a jab, Jackson unleashed another crushing right hand that landed flush on McKnight's jaw, sending him to the canvas again.

A smart fighter doesn't jump up immediately after being knocked down; he's still groggy, akin to someone who's had too much to drink. Rising too quickly can cause a stumble, leading the referee to stop the fight. McKnight, now on one knee for the second time in less than a minute, glanced at me in the corner with a look of frustration.

In desperation, I shouted, "You've got to take it

to him. You've got to fight him!"

When the referee resumed the bout, hundreds of hometown fans began chanting, "Keith! Keith! Keith!" Energized, McKnight went straight at Jackson, pushing him across the ring before the fighters clinched. McKnight wisely used the clinch to clear his head, allowing the round to end.

Mark Frazie, a former world-class middleweight boxer who had helped train McKnight for this bout, assisted me in the corner. We worked to calm McKnight. It was only the second round, and we reassured him that he had plenty of time to win. We sponged cold water over his head, neck, and body, washed out his mouthpiece, massaged him, and gave him water to drink.

When the bell sounded for the third round, the crowd began chanting "Keith! Keith! Keith!" again revitalizing McKnight. He soon found his rhythm, moving around the ring like a master matador, landing his left jab with precision—pop, pop, pop! As the rounds progressed, McKnight began catching Jackson with clean combinations—bing, bing, bing, bing! Boom! He was stinging and frustrating Jackson, who, in desperation, swung wildly, trying to land a knockout punch.

McKnight, younger, faster, and more mobile, evaded Jackson's big bombs and countered effectively. Every time Jackson loaded up and threw one of those bombs, McKnight slipped away and returned fire, catching the angry, frustrated Jackson clean. As the fight wore on, McKnight took control, winning the bout with his smooth, graceful boxing skills. Between the ninth and tenth rounds, Jackson's Cuban trainer slapped him in the face and screamed that he was losing the fight, telling him, "You've got to knock him out to win!"

In the tenth round, Jackson came out looking for a knockout. But McKnight, in a graceful rhythm, continued to land fast, clean shots, maneuvering out of harm's way. The final bell rang, and the judges tallied their scorecards—McKnight had won a unanimous decision against the most dangerous fighter he had ever faced. For those who said McKnight had beaten a faded fighter, Jackson went on to knock out his next six consecutive opponents.

I was incredibly proud of Keith that night. It was a tough, hard fight, but he had prevailed. I believed this win would give McKnight the confidence to beat anyone in the world.

During World War II, British Prime Minister Sir Winston Churchill said, "Never, never, never, never, never give up." Great Britain didn't give up and eventually prevailed against Nazi Germany's onslaught and their evil leader, Adolf Hitler.

McKnight embodied Churchill's words when he picked himself up off the floor, not once, but twice, to defeat the formidable Phil Jackson. That night was McKnight's finest hour as a professional boxer—he simply wouldn't give up.

To this day, I remain proud of Keith McKnight for overcoming his doubts, refusing to give up, and defeating Phil Jackson, a boxer with killer power.

— 17 —

Benito "Baby" Ortiz: From the Ring to Redemption

Benito Ortiz

Benito "Benny" Ortiz was a world-class featherweight boxer in the 1960s, rising to prominence as a stablemate of three-time world champion Emile Griffith. Managed by the legendary Boxing Hall of Fame trainer Gil Clancy, Benny's talent and charisma earned him four appearances at the iconic Madison Square Garden in New York City. Known for his smooth, fluid style, Benny described his unique approach to boxing as "Spanish dancing." During his fighting days, he was affectionately nicknamed "Baby" Ortiz.

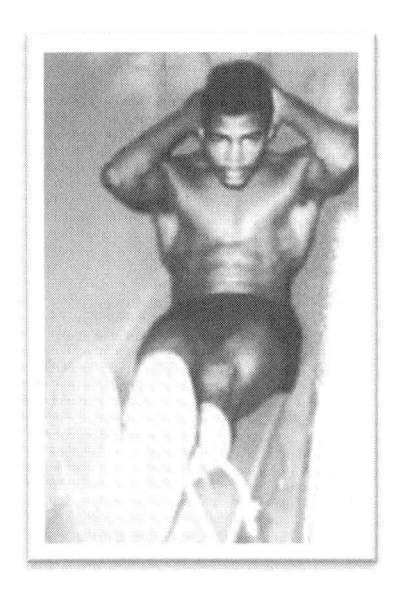

Benito Ortiz in a pre-bout workout

After hanging up his gloves, Benny transitioned into a career as a professional boxing trainer in his native Puerto Rico. He later became the head trainer and manager of the renowned Times Square Gym in New York, which was owned by his former trainer, Jimmy Glenn. Benny's specialty as a trainer was teaching boxers to glide effortlessly around the ring, incorporating his "Spanish dancing" style of movement. In training sessions, he would use salsa dance steps to demonstrate how to pivot, move in and out, and maneuver around the ring with grace.

Benito helped develop two of my protégés, Ken Atkin, who won a WBF light-heavyweight championship and finished his career with a respectable 30-5 record, and Keith McKnight, a quick and mobile heavyweight who achieved more than 40 wins in his career. Whenever Bobby Goodman, the matchmaker at Madison Square Garden, had fighters preparing for bouts at the famed venue, he would send them to Benny for training while they were in New York.

Benny earned a reputation as a wild man during his boxing days. He was known for his love of partying, drinking, gambling, and dancing all night in the Puerto Rican clubs of Spanish Harlem. Some who knew him back then recall that Benny had no hesitation in settling disputes with a gun or a knife if necessary.

However, Benny's life took a dramatic turn one early morning in 1992. After staggering home from a night of heavy drinking and partying, he was suddenly overwhelmed with a deep sense of guilt about the way he was living. He realized that his lifestyle was putting him in danger of losing his beloved wife, Sonja, and their two sons, Benito Jr. and Owen. In a moment of reflection, Benny turned on the radio and heard a preacher urging listeners to give their lives to Jesus Christ. The preacher invited the audience to pray and ask Christ for salvation. At 4 a.m., Benito called the preacher and said, "My name is Benito Ortiz, and I need to get saved." As the preacher prayed with him, Benito gave his life to Christ.

Kerry Pharr, Benito Ortiz (2023)

From that day on, Benny never looked back. Interestingly, Benito and his family lived in a New York apartment next door to the mother of former world champion Hector "Macho" Camacho. Benny left his job at New York's Times Square Gym and gave up drinking, gambling, and street fighting. He dedicated his life to sharing the story of how Christ transformed him. Today, Benito is a joyful disciple of Christ, living with a radiant smile, a happy bounce in his step, and a deep love for others. Benito and his sons are happily married and now live in Florida. He remains very active in his church, preaching and singing whenever he is called upon.

— 18 —

Eddie Futch's First Boxer: Luthur Burgess

Most boxing fans are familiar with the legendary trainer Eddie Futch, who guided 21 world champions, including five heavyweight champions, to greatness. However, the name Luther Burgess might not ring as many bells. Luther, a featherweight boxer from 1946 to 1949, was the very first professional fighter that Eddie Futch trained.

Back in the summer of 1997, I had the privilege of speaking with Luther about his early days in boxing. Neither of us could have known that tragedy would soon strike us both in ways we could never have imagined. Luther began our conversation by reminiscing about the day Eddie Futch first noticed him. As a teenager, Luther was playing baseball when Eddie called out to him, "Hey kid, when you're done playing, come see me, and I'll teach you how to box."

Luther said, "There was something about the way

he said it that really got to me." He added with a smile, "You know, you can play basketball, you can play football, and you can play baseball, but you can't play boxing."

Luther eventually gave up baseball and allowed Eddie to shape him into a skilled professional boxer. In those days, fighters weren't protected, so when an opportunity arose to make money, they took it. In Luther's eighth, ninth, and tenth professional fights, he faced a top featherweight contender and two future hall-of-fame world champions. Remarkably, these fights took place within just four months.

Luther Burgess, Keith McKnight, Kerry Pharr (1997)

On April 4, 1948, Luther defeated top featherweight contender Jock Leslie in a 10-round decision. Two months later, on June 25, Luther faced the legendary featherweight world champion Willie

"Will o' the Wisp" Pep, whose record was an astounding 126-1 at the time. In only his ninth professional fight, Luther went the distance with Pep, ultimately losing a 10-round decision to the future hall-of-famer.

Just a month later, Luther and Eddie arrived in New Orleans from Detroit to face future lightweight champion Joe "Old Bones" Brown. Once again, Luther went the distance, earning a respectable draw with the future champion. After five more fights, Luther retired from boxing in 1949.

Following his retirement, Luther naturally transitioned into a boxing trainer. Those who knew him well believe that he could have become as renowned as Eddie Futch or Emanuel Steward if not for some personal challenges. In fact, many who worked closely with Luther argue that he was an exceptional trainer. During his years at Detroit's famous Kronk Gym, Luther played a significant role in the development of many highly accomplished boxers, contributing greatly to Kronk's impressive legacy.

Around the same time Luther shared his early boxing memories with me in 1997, I was managing and training a quick, mobile heavyweight named Keith McKnight. I felt that Keith needed a great trainer to help him reach the next level, and I believed that even a slight improvement could earn us a shot at the heavyweight championship.

Although Emanuel Steward was training Lennox Lewis at the time, making it unlikely we could secure his services, I had become friends with Luther and decided to ask for his help.

When I first approached Luther by phone about training McKnight, he declined. Determined, Keith and I flew from Nashville to Detroit to speak with Luther in person. We invited him to watch Keith spar with Buster Mathis Jr. in Grand Rapids, Michigan. That day, Keith looked phenomenal, impressing Luther enough that he reconsidered and agreed to work with us. However, because Luther was still employed by Emanuel Steward at Kronk Gym and had a deep respect for Steward, he needed to ensure Emanuel's support before committing.

We arranged a lunch with the charismatic Emanuel Steward so Luther could request permission to help McKnight. Emanuel graciously gave his blessing, expressing happiness for Luther's opportunity to make some money. He even allowed McKnight to train at Kronk Gym for his first fight under Luther's guidance. On May 1, 1997, in Asbury Park, New Jersey, Keith won a unanimous 10-round decision against Ed Donaldson, with HBO commentator Harold Lederman praising Luther Burgess's exceptional work in McKnight's corner.

For McKnight's second fight with Luther, we trained at Roy Jones Jr.'s gym in Pensacola, Florida. Former cruiserweight world champion Al Cole was also training there, preparing for his own bout. Roy's company, Square Ring, and Coach Alton Merkelson generously provided us with accommodations and excellent sparring opportunities with Cole.

After our time in Pensacola, we returned to Nashville, where Luther, who had grown up in the South, enjoyed our southern hospitality. We made sure he had all his favorite southern dishes, from gravy and biscuits to fried chicken and banana pudding. Luther seemed to have a wonderful time in Nashville; I can still picture him relaxing in a lounge chair under a shade tree in my backyard, taking a nap after a satisfying meal.

After our brief stay in Nashville, we flew to Lewiston, Idaho, where Keith faced Bryan Scott in a 10-round main event on the Nez Perce Indian reservation. In this second fight under Luther's tutelage, Keith won decisively, stopping Scott in the first round. Luther had prepared Keith exceptionally well for both fights, and the future looked promising for Team McKnight.

Unfortunately, just a day after returning home to Detroit, Luther went out to celebrate the win. The following morning, the 70-year-old trainer suffered a stroke that left him paralyzed and unable to speak. In September, my first wife, Diane, and I flew to Detroit to visit Luther in the hospital. We prayed with him and spent time expressing our deep affection for him. Tragically, shortly after our return to Nashville,

Diane was diagnosed with breast cancer. Luther passed away a few months later, and my beloved wife Diane succumbed to her illness four years after that.

Having had the opportunity to know and work with Luther Burgess was a tremendous blessing in my life. Luther was a great father, a loving husband, an outstanding boxing trainer, and a true friend. Rest in peace, Luther.

— 19 —

The Tragic Tale of Big John Tate

Around that time, John Tate, the former heavyweight champion of the world, had lost his title and spiraled into a dark world of addiction and crime. He became addicted to cocaine, committed numerous petty crimes, and even broke a man's jaw in a street fight. His downward spiral landed him in Brushy Mountain State Prison in Tennessee. One night, Billy Collins Sr. came to my Club Knockout Boxing Gym and encouraged me to visit Tate in prison, suggesting I offer him help upon his release. I had known Tate's manager and trainer, Ace Miller, and had sent sparring partners to work with Tate when he was still boxing. John and I were acquainted long before his incarceration.

Determined to help, I reached out to Tate and got myself added to his approved visitor list. I made the drive to Brushy Mountain State Prison, named after the rugged mountains of East Tennessee, where it was located. Tate was thrilled when I offered him a lifeline: a place to live, a gym to train in, and a promotional contract to resume his boxing career. He was due for release soon and assured me, "I'll call you as soon as I'm out, and we'll get started." A few weeks later, I received a collect call from John Tate. He was at the Knoxville courthouse, awaiting his release. "I'll call you later today after I see the judge, and you can come get me," he said. I was excited, eager to work with the former champ. But the call never came.

John Tate with Bernard Taylor (1979)

John got caught up in the streets once more, becoming a vagrant, working odd jobs, pan-handling and committing petty crimes to survive.

Six years passed, and during that time, Keith McKnight had risen in the boxing world, boasting an impressive record of 33 wins with just one loss. He was on a hot streak, with 4 consecutive victories, and his next bout was set to be televised nationally on USA's *Tuesday Night Fights*. He would be facing Obed Sullivan, the world's fourth-ranked heavyweight in the world—a pivotal moment in his career. The great trainer Luther Burgess had died, and I was looking for someone who might fill his shoes to continue developing McKnight.

As we trained for the fight at Horace Kent's gym in Knoxville, Tennessee, an unexpected figure walked through the doors—Big John Tate, the former heavyweight champion. I had known John for nearly 20 years, back when Ace Miller had expertly managed his career and guided him to the pinnacle of boxing. But those days were long gone. Despite earning around $2 million in the ring, John had lost everything to drug abuse and petty crime. His money, home, cars—all gone. Even worse, his wife had left him, and his once-glorious reputation was in ruins.

Hearing about McKnight's upcoming televised fight, John asked if he could help us prepare Keith for the big event. Despite his troubled past, McKnight and I decided to take a chance on Tate. We brought him back to our base in the Nashville area, where he stayed in a small apartment behind the gym for six weeks leading up to the fight. Most people lock their doors at night for safety, but not Big John. He slept soundly with the door wide open—a stark reminder of how much he had lost and how little he had left to lose.

People who knew John's history were skeptical. "Why do you have that crackhead working with you?" they would ask. But I saw it as an opportunity—for McKnight to learn from a former world champion and for John to find a way back from the brink. Despite everything, there were still moments when people recognized him, asking, "Aren't you Big John Tate, the former heavyweight champion of the world?" And with a glimmer of pride, John would reply, "Yeah! I was the baddest man on the planet for a minute." Unfortunately, Tate was more of a problem than he was helpful. We never saw any indication of drug use while we were prepping for the Sullivan fight, but we missed the sage advice and knowledge of Luther Burgess. Not only for McKnight but for me as well.[1]

A couple of days before the fight, our team flew

---

[1] Here's a link to a video on my YouTube channel showing McKnight sparring Shazzon Bradley, with John Tate and me standing on the left side of the ring that very night of January 2, 1998. Tate is in the center and I'm in the left corner. Tate was coaching McKnight's sparring partner, Bradley. https://www.youtube.com/watch?v=el-6seiqAas. In addition, you can find a YouTube link of a video of Luther working with McKnight: https://www.youtube.com/watch?v=RiMKMZ3N5dw

to Connecticut for the weigh-in and pre-fight physicals. After the bout with Sullivan, McKnight lost to a fighter I believe he could have beaten. I was broken-hearted since I had spent ten years of my life working nearly every day with Keith and I loved him like a son. In my heart, I knew that this was his last shot at "Big Time" boxing and the financial opportunities that would have brought us. Immediately after the fight, our promoter dropped us like a hot potato. It was a very discouraging time for Team McKnight.

When we returned to Nashville I paid Tate his cut in cash—he had thousands of dollars in his pocket. At the airport John wasn't scheduled to leave for Knoxville for several hours, so he asked me to drop him off in downtown Nashville. When he requested to be let out at the housing projects on Lafayette Street, I couldn't shake a feeling of dread. I asked if he was sure, and he nodded. I feared the worst—that he was heading there to buy drugs—but there was nothing more I could do. We said our goodbyes, and that was the last time I ever saw the champ.

Six weeks later, tragedy struck. Big John was driving a pickup truck when an undiagnosed brain tumor compressed an artery at the base of his skull. The truck slammed into a telephone pole, killing him almost instantly. He was just 43 years old. The medical examiner said he had ingested cocaine within the last twelve hours of his life.

Big John Tate's life is a tragic tale of glory and downfall—a man who once stood at the top of the world, only to be brought low by the weight of his addiction. He was the baddest man on the planet for a minute, but in the end, he became just another lost soul, searching for redemption in a world that had long forgotten his name.

— 20 —

Mark Gastineau: Pro Football's King of the Sack

Mark Gastineau, a former All-Pro defensive end in the NFL, played for the New York Jets from 1979 to 1988. Known for his aggressive pass rushing, he amassed 100.5 quarterback sacks in his first 100 starts. In 1984, Gastineau set a single-season sack record with 22 sacks, a record that held for 16 years until Michael Strahan of the New York Giants controversially broke it in 2001, with many believing that Green Bay quarterback Brett Favre had allowed Strahan to sack him.

After retiring from football, Gastineau pursued a career in professional boxing. His handlers aimed to leverage his fame by building an impressive boxing record against carefully chosen opponents, all with the ultimate goal of arranging a lucrative fight against former heavyweight champion George Foreman. Gastineau's sheer size, strength, and athleticism could have secured him some victories, even with minimal training. However, those around him manipulated him, convincing him that he was a skilled boxer, all while orchestrating his matches to secure a big payday.

Two years into Gastineau's boxing career, I found myself unwittingly involved in a fixed fight featuring him. In the spring of 1993, Randall "Tex" Cobb, a former heavyweight boxing contender and character actor, began training at Club Knockout, a boxing gym I managed in Nashville. Cobb, who had been retired for several years, was on a comeback trail, hoping to fight his way back into heavyweight title contention.

Cobb's first boxing career was marked by a one-sided fight against heavyweight champion Larry Holmes, a bout so lopsided that ringside announcer Howard Cosell famously quit boxing commentary in protest. Despite lacking technical skills, Cobb was known for his incredible toughness and durability, traits that allowed him to survive Holmes' relentless attacks without ever going down. Cobb's fights were always grueling, and he was one of the toughest men to ever step into the ring.

During his training at Club Knockout, Cobb expressed interest in fighting again in a main event in Nashville. He mentioned that his manager, Rick Parker, who also managed heavyweight contender "Smokin'" Bert Cooper and Gastineau, wanted to promote a show in Nashville. Parker didn't have a promoter's license in Tennessee, so he needed a local promoter to co-host the event. Although I had heard that Parker was not the most trustworthy person, I was excited about the opportunity to be involved in a promotion featuring well-known boxers like Cobb, Cooper, and Gastineau. After speaking with Parker on the phone, we agreed to co-promote the event, with me using my promoter's license. In return, Parker promised to feature Cobb in the main event, Cooper in an exhibition, and Gastineau in an undercard bout, along with my boxer, Keith McKnight. We agreed to split the profits 50-50.

Over the next six weeks, I worked tirelessly to promote the show, which was shaping up to be a major success. Cobb continued to train at our gym, and ticket sales were strong. However, just a week before the event, Cobb mysteriously withdrew from the fight, despite being in good health. I was baffled by his decision, but Parker assured me that everything would still go according to plan.

As the event approached, Parker and his entourage, including Cooper and Gastineau, arrived in Nashville. At our gym, Cooper sparred with one of our heavyweights, while Gastineau's trainer had him work on the hand mitts, avoiding sparring altogether. It was clear to everyone that Gastineau was a novice boxer, and local pros even asked me for a chance to fight him, eager to add his name to their records. I felt sorry for Gastineau, who seemed unaware that his handlers were exploiting him for a payday without properly developing his boxing skills.

The event took place on June 18, 1993, at Nashville's Municipal Auditorium. Parker had arranged for Billy Mitchem, a well-known and lifelong boxing manager, to bring an opponent for Gastineau—Terry Miller, a fighter with a record of 0 wins and 10 losses. Gastineau, with a record of 14-1 against handpicked opponents, faced off against Miller. The crowd cheered as the match began, but it quickly became evident that Miller was outclassing Gastineau. Miller won the first two rounds and was dominating the third when, suddenly and without any apparent reason, he fell to the mat and didn't get up. The referee counted to ten, and Gastineau was credited with another knockout. The crowd, sensing foul play, began chanting "bullshit" in unison.

After the event, Parker collected the gate proceeds and assured me we would settle later. However, I never saw or heard from him again. The loss of my share of the profits was nothing compared to the damage done to my reputation by being associated with Parker and the promotion.

On October 4, 1993, *Sports Illustrated* published an article titled "The Fix Was In," accusing Parker of fixing fights in favor of Cobb and Gastineau. Although there was no concrete proof, it suddenly made sense to me why Cobb had withdrawn from the fight. Cobb later won a lawsuit against *Sports*

Illustrated for defamation, although the decision was overturned on appeal.

While Gastineau may not have known he was fighting less-than-formidable opponents, the *Sports Illustrated* article suggested he was aware of the match-fixing. The story of Rick Parker came to a tragic end on April 28, 1995, when he was shot and killed by Tim "Doc" Anderson, a professional boxer whom Parker had allegedly poisoned before a match against Gastineau. Anderson claimed that Parker had stolen his earnings, used them for drugs, and even arranged for him to be beaten by thugs when Anderson refused to take a dive against Gastineau.

Anderson, who later shot Parker in self-defense after Parker threatened his disabled sister, was convicted of premeditated first-degree murder and sentenced to life without parole. Many believe Anderson's trial was unfair, and he has since been incarcerated in a Florida prison.

— 21 —

Slaves of the Sugar Plantation

In August 2001, I embarked on a sports mission trip to the Dominican Republic, an island nation in the Caribbean Sea, nestled between Cuba and Puerto Rico. Joining me on this journey were professional boxer Warren Williams, known for his bouts against former heavyweight champions James "Buster" Douglas and Shannon Briggs, and amateur boxers Jake Thomas and Robert Crutcher. Williams, a journeyman boxer with a heart of gold, brought a unique and inspiring presence to our mission.

This trip was organized by SCORE International, a sports ministry founded in 1985 by Ron Bishop, the former head basketball coach at Tennessee Temple University in Chattanooga. Bishop left coaching to pursue his passion for evangelism through sports. SCORE International's mission is to spread the gospel through sporting events and community service.

During our time in the Dominican Republic, we

visited local boxing gyms, baseball parks, and recreation centers. Our boxers would spar with local athletes, and afterward, we shared the gospel with them. We also traveled with other college-aged basketball and volleyball teams, all under the direction of SCORE International. These teams played against Dominican all-star teams, using the games as a platform to preach the Gospel of Jesus Christ to the local communities.

Warren Williams, Jake Thomas, Robert Crutcher

Sports, particularly baseball, hold a special place in the hearts of the Dominican people. Baseball is a national passion, and any Dominican you ask will proudly recount a list of the country's greatest players. During our trip, we visited the capital, Santo Domingo, and spent several days in San Pedro, the hometown of baseball legend Sammy Sosa. The country is breathtaking, with unspoiled nature, a thousand miles of coastline, white sandy beaches, and turquoise waters.

On our first evening there, just before dusk, Warren and I decided to wade into the beautiful sea, unaware of the danger lurking beneath the waves. As we ventured waist-deep, the 6'1", 240-pound Williams suddenly screamed in pain. His eyes filled with terror, and I rushed to help him, only to experience the same excruciating pain. We had both stepped on sea urchins the size of softballs, and their spines had pierced the soles of our feet, causing a burning sensation. The pain was intense. For the rest of our trip, we tried in vain to remove the spines with tweezers, only to learn later that this was the wrong approach. The spines, being living tissue, break off when pulled. The best way to remove them, as we discovered later, is by pouring melted wax onto the skin and peeling it away once it hardens.

Despite this painful experience, the Dominican people were incredibly receptive to our message. After each game or sparring session, they would gather on the basketball court or baseball field to listen attentively to our message of hope. One native, who lived in New York City but was vacationing in his homeland, approached me after I spoke to a group of locals. "Sir," he said, "I want to thank you for coming to my country and telling my people about

Jesus Christ."

Haiti, located on the western third of Hispaniola, has many citizens who sneak across the border to work in the sugar cane fields of the Dominican Republic. Although they may resemble some Dominicans, their dialect is distinctly different, a legacy of the island's colonial past—Haiti was a French colony, while the Dominican Republic was Spanish. The Dominicans try to prevent the Haitians from integrating into their society, and once they cross the border, they are often not allowed to return to Haiti. Many times, the Haitian government refuses to accept them back, leaving them as a people without a country.

During our stay, our missionary hosts took all the sports teams to visit a sugar cane village. These villages are miserable labor camps where numerous human rights abuses occur. The Haitians, forced to work in the sugar cane fields to survive, live in tattered shacks and earn a meager $5-10 per day. The conditions were appalling—no running water, no indoor plumbing, and abject poverty. They were, in essence, slaves.

In the village, I noticed a company store owned by the sugar plantation, stocked almost entirely with hard liquor. "What heartless bloodsuckers," I thought. It was bad enough that the plantation owners paid these poor people slave wages, but to then sell them alcohol to drown their sorrows was beyond

- cruel.

I encountered a beautiful little girl, about four years old, who clung to her mother's leg, frightened and shy. One of the basketball coaches told me that he had visited the village two years earlier. The mother had begged him to take her daughter to the United States, where she could have a better life. The coach had wanted to help, but when the mother asked him to take the little girl, she began to cry hysterically and clung tightly to her mother.

There is so much sadness and inhumanity in the world today. I often wish I could do more to help those less fortunate than myself. My desire is to share the Word of God, offering hope to those living in hopeless situations.

I have produced a documentary titled *Forgotten No More*, highlighting the slavery-like conditions in the Dominican Republic. We want to share this important story with you. If you would like to see the film for free, please visit www.InYourCorner.tv.

— 22 —

Boxing's Treacherous Road

For those new to the world of managing or training professional boxers, the manager's main objective is to help a fighter reach their full potential. Young men eager to enter the professional ranks of boxing must be aware of several crucial aspects before starting their careers.

Most professional boxers have amateur experience before turning pro. The best professionals often start young, some as early as 8 or 10 years old, gaining years of experience by the time they are 18-20. Legends like Muhammad Ali, Sugar Ray Leonard, Thomas "Hit Man" Hearns, and Oscar De La Hoya all began as young amateurs. By the time they went professional, they had fought in at least 150 amateur bouts, winning numerous local, regional, and national championships. Leonard and De La Hoya even claimed Olympic gold at the Montreal and Los Angeles Olympics, respectively. If a boxer has limited experience, competing against fighters with this level of background will be a steep challenge.

These seasoned fighters have honed their skills through countless championships during their teenage years, making them formidable opponents. The best strategy for an aspiring boxer is to stay in the amateur ranks until they have enough experience to compete at a high level. Success as an amateur often lays the groundwork for success as a professional. If you can't win a local Golden Gloves tournament, turning professional might be premature.

A loss in amateur boxing doesn't significantly hurt a fighter's value, but a loss in the professional arena can severely impact a career. An undefeated professional boxer holds more value than one with losses. However, it's important not to judge a fighter solely by their record. A boxer with a poor record may be tough, while one with an impressive record might have faced weaker opponents.

A skilled boxer who turns professional is known as a prospect. If they remain undefeated after fifteen or sixteen bouts, they're seen as a strong prospect. However, if they lose several bouts, they are relegated to the status of an opponent, the kind of fighter used to build up the records of other prospects.

Developing a boxer from an amateur to a prospect, then into a contender, and ultimately a world champion, is a process. A prospect is usually untested, having won bouts against weaker opponents. To progress from being a prospect to a contender, a fighter must defeat a fellow contender or win a regional title like the Continental Americas Championship, United States Boxing Association, or North American Boxing Federation championship against a worthy opponent. These regional titles are steppingstones to a world title.

A contender is someone capable of competing against the world champion. Climbing the ranks in professional boxing is a step-by-step process. The ultimate goal for any boxing manager or trainer is to help their boxer win a world championship and earn millions, securing financial stability for both the boxer and the manager.

However, the reality is that very few fighters earn the kind of money that superstars do. Only about two percent of professional boxers make significant money from the sport. The number of million-dollar fighters is small.

As a boxing manager, trainer, and promoter for over 20 years, I never earned enough to quit my day job. None of the fighters I managed became famous or made enough to retire comfortably. The biggest payday my fighters usually saw was between $20,000-$25,000, with my share as a manager being one-third of the purse. After covering the trainer's expenses, the cut-man's expenses, and other costs, I often ended up spending more money on the boxers than I made. Most trainers and managers work in boxing for the love of the sport, the athletes, and the occasional recognition.

In the early stages, most debuting professional boxers who haven't won an Olympic gold medal fight for as little as $100 per round, or $400 for a four-round fight. After deducting license fees and the manager and trainer's percentages, the boxer is left with even less. Many managers are notorious for exploiting their fighters.

I once worked with a Cuban manager who brought fighters from Latin America, putting them in tough fights to maximize his earnings. He would pay the fighter a small fraction of the purse while pocketing the rest. This kind of exploitation is not only immoral but criminal. Although federal laws like the Muhammad Ali Act have been enacted to prevent such exploitation, similar practices still occur in professional boxing today.

If you're a young man aspiring to box professionally, choose your manager wisely. Ensure they are someone who won't exploit you and understands how to develop and advance your career. A good manager will invest thousands, even hundreds of thousands of dollars over several years without taking a percentage of the boxer's purse until the purses are large enough to justify it.

Most second and third tier boxers can't earn a living from boxing alone in the early stages of their careers. Many have full-time jobs, using boxing to supplement their income. The same goes for most trainers and managers, who also work full-time jobs while managing and training boxers part-time. These working-class managers and trainers can't afford to subsidize their fighters or pay for top-notch sparring partners like the champions do.

Developing a professional boxer is a slow, arduous process. You have to book your fighter on other promoters' boxing cards or become a promoter yourself. If you choose the former, the odds are against you. Your athlete becomes a road warrior, fighting on other promoters' shows, usually against their house fighters in their hometowns. Local fighters have the advantage of a supportive fan base, and local judges may be biased in favor of the hometown boxer.

In many ways, developing a professional boxer is like playing chess. One wrong move can end your fighter's career. Maneuvering a boxer through the ranks can feel like swimming in shark-infested waters, with promoters and managers constantly trying to poach your fighter.

Imagine you're a boxing manager, and your goal is to keep your athlete undefeated while climbing the ranks. An undefeated fighter can command much more money than one with losses. As a manager, you spend years and thousands of dollars trying to keep your fighter undefeated, aiming for a world championship and a big payday. Along the way, you face tough fighters, promoters, and matchmakers who take satisfaction in getting your fighter beaten.

Teddy Brenner, the famous Madison Square Garden matchmaker, was known for his ability to get any fighter beaten. Even the greatest fighters, like Muhammad Ali, needed time to develop their skills after leaving the amateur ranks and entering the professional world.

— 23 —

Dave Wolf, the Epitome of a Great Boxing Manager

Dave Wolf, a former *Life Magazine* sportswriter and one of the most accomplished boxing managers in history, was a true master at developing fighters. He worked with heavyweight champion Joe Frazier and managed the careers of several notable athletes, including former Olympian and top heavyweight contender Duane Bobick, football legend Ed "Too Tall" Jones, and world champions such as Ray "Boom Boom" Mancini, Louis Espinoza, Donnie LaLonde, and Lonnie Bradley. Wolf's success lay in his brilliance as a negotiator.

I had the privilege of working with Dave Wolf for several years, and during that time, I featured some of his boxers on my professional boxing shows. His former champion, Donnie Lalonde, also trained at our gym for one of his fights, and I helped secure opponents for his last world championship and worked in the corner of his champion, Lonnie

Bradley. I spent countless hours listening to Wolf as we traveled together on numerous boxing trips, and he became an incredible mentor to me concerning the business side of boxing. While he may not have been an expert on the fighters themselves, he had a deep understanding of the business aspect of the sport. His expertise was so sharp that he managed to secure a fight for Lalonde against the legendary Sugar Ray Leonard, which resulted in a seven-million-dollar payday. I can attest to this because he not only told me how he orchestrated it, but he also showed me the canceled check for seven million dollars.

A good manager protects his fighter but also challenges him by gradually moving him up against better competition. On the other hand, a boxing matchmaker's job is to create competitive bouts that excite the fans. Matchmakers often undersell opponents to managers, leading them to believe the fight is easier than it actually is. Once in the ring, the opponent might turn out to be much tougher than expected.

As a manager, you often find yourself in an adversarial role with promoters and matchmakers. Once your fighter is capable of fighting a 10-round main event, you can usually secure a contract with a major promoter for televised fights. However, promoters often sign multiple fighters in the same weight division, creating a situation where they pit their own boxers against each other. This makes the role of a promoter somewhat contradictory, as they are supposed to promote their fighters but often end up eliminating them in the process.

Boxing is a complex and challenging sport, not just in the ring but also in the business side. For those involved, it's a treacherous road filled with challenges, tough decisions, and the constant threat of exploitation. But for those who navigate it successfully, the rewards—both personal and financial—can be significant.

— 24 —

Fight the Good Fight

I spent 38 years of my life in boxing. I started in the gym as an amateur boxer at 14 years of age and left the sport as a professional boxing manager, trainer, and promoter in 2001 after my first wife died of breast cancer. Over the years I trained hundreds of amateurs and too many professionals to count.

Throughout my career, I've had the privilege of managing and training two intercontinental champions and one world champion. Ken Atkin secured the WBF light-heavyweight title in a hard-fought victory against Mexico's Carlos Cantu. Darrell "Fast Fists" Fuller claimed the WBC Continental Americas Championship, while Keith McKnight won the WBF Heavyweight Intercontinental Championship and fought for the N.A.B.F. Heavyweight title. McKnight also delivered knockout victories over former world champions J.B. Williamson and Iran Barkley.

Despite often being seen as underdogs, my

fighters have faced some of the toughest names in the sport. I've worked the corner against six heavyweight champions. Warren Williams, for example, took on James "Buster" Douglas, the first man to knock out Mike Tyson, and later squared off against Shannon Briggs in a high-profile Cedric Kushner promotion in New York City.

Another fighter I managed, Kenny Merritt, fought Tommy Morrison in a nationally televised bout and later battled Lou Savarese in Reno. Savarese went on to win the IBA World Heavyweight title by knocking out former Undisputed World Heavyweight Champion Buster Douglas in the first round. Despite his challenges, Merritt also engaged in an intense eight-round war against Brian Nielsen in Denmark, with Nielsen eventually becoming the IBO heavyweight champion. I was in the corner in every one of these matches as well hundreds more.

A decade after stepping away from the boxing world, I embarked on a new journey as an international television host on the faith-based Daystar TV Network, which reached audiences in 500 countries worldwide. My show, fittingly named *In Your Corner with Kerry Pharr,* became a platform for more than 500 episodes, where I had the privilege of interviewing many athletes who were also men of faith.

Two of my most cherished projects include a

captivating 51-minute interview with Evander Holyfield, one of the greatest heavyweight champions of all time. In this candid conversation, Evander shares some remarkable stories, including his thoughts on the infamous moment when Mike Tyson bit off a piece of his ear and what their relationship is like today.[2]

While producing *In Your Corner,* I had the honor of interviewing numerous former boxing and kickboxing contenders and world champions who were devout followers of Jesus Christ. Some of the incredible athletes who shared their stories with me include Evander Holyfield, eight-time world champion boxer and kickboxer Troy Dorsey, Kickboxing Champion Bernard "Swift Kick" Robinson, former Junior Welterweight Champion Gene "Mad Dog" Hatcher, former WBF Champion Ken "The Bull" Atkin, and former world title challenger and one of the most decorated amateur boxers ever, Jerome "Kid" Coffee.

Additionally, I spoke with stars of NBC's *The Contender Series,* world title challenger Johnathon Reid, Anthony "Brent" Cooper, and Adam Richards, who won four national amateur championships and

---

[2] Here is a video link where you can watch it free: https://youtu.be/mq1V-YQKT6k?si=idxl_QOT17XjNwgo

one world amateur championship. Richards, along with Mike Tyson, is one of the only boxers to win two Junior Olympic national titles by knocking out every opponent both years.

We compiled these remarkable stories into a 58-minute documentary titled *Fight the Good Fight*. While it may cost to watch on streaming platforms, I want you to enjoy it for free. See the link below.[3]

---

[3] Here's the link:
https://youtu.be/Z3SJJ7v8RdU?si=1ystNRR06ZXXB8V5

— 25 —

From Death to Life

There was a time in my life when I was speeding down a dead-end street at ninety miles an hour, lost in a wild and reckless lifestyle filled with drugs, alcohol, and all the chaos that comes with it. Despite the constant whirlwind, I was empty, miserable, and my life felt utterly meaningless. Then someone shared a Bible passage with me and revealed a truth that changed everything: **Jesus Christ voluntarily gave His life to save not just me, but everyone willing to accept His free gift of salvation.**

I discovered the incredible news of Jesus' life—born of a virgin, living a perfect life, and willingly dying on the cross to save humanity from the punishment of sin. Accepting Jesus Christ is as simple as A, B, C:

A. Admit that you are a sinner. "For all have sinned and come short of the glory of God." Romans 3:23
B. Believe that Jesus paid the penalty for your sins

on the cross. "For God so loved the world, that He gave His only Son, that whoever believes in Him should not perish, but have everlasting life." John 3:16

C. Confess that Jesus is Lord, and simply ask Him to forgive your sins and save your soul. "That if thou shalt confess with thy mouth the Lord Jesus, and shalt believe in thine heart that God hath raised Him from the dead, thou shalt be saved. For with the heart man believeth unto righteousness; and with the mouth confession is made unto salvation." Romans 10:9, 10

I hope that you will ask Jesus into your life and know the joy and peace of a life that comes by serving Him. If you would like to contact me, please connect with me at my website:

www.InYourCorner.tv

We currently do a weekly Livestream at my Facebook and YouTube pages. Here's the link for the weekly Livestream:

FaceBook.com/Kerry Pharr
https://www.youtube.com/@InYourCornerMin/streams

Visit our Facebook or YouTube page to see when our next Livestream is being sent to YOU!

Made in the USA
Columbia, SC
28 October 2024